William Sanday

The Conception of Priesthood in the Early Church and in the Church of England

of England

Four Sermons. Second Edition

William Sanday

The Conception of Priesthood in the Early Church and in the Church of England
Four Sermons. Second Edition

ISBN/EAN: 9783744708531

Printed in Europe, USA, Canada, Australia, Japan

Cover: Foto ©Lupo / pixelio.de

More available books at **www.hansebooks.com**

THE
CONCEPTION OF PRIESTHOOD

THE

CONCEPTION OF PRIESTHOOD
IN THE EARLY CHURCH

AND IN THE

CHURCH OF ENGLAND

Four Sermons

BY

W. SANDAY, D.D., LL.D.

LADY MARGARET PROFESSOR OF DIVINITY AND CANON OF CHRIST CHURCH
HONORARY FELLOW OF EXETER COLLEGE

SECOND EDITION

WITH NEW PREFACE AND TWO APPENDICES

LONGMANS, GREEN, AND CO.

39 PATERNOSTER ROW, LONDON

NEW YORK AND BOMBAY

1899

Oxford

HORACE HART, PRINTER TO THE UNIVERSITY

PREFACE

TO THE SECOND EDITION

THE second edition which has been called for of this book will have an unusual advantage. Through the kindness of Dr. Moberly and of the editor of the *Guardian*, I am allowed to print with it, in the form of appendices, a searching, if at the same time a very indulgent, examination of the book itself, along with some words of my own in reply. I do not attempt to answer every point that has been raised, or that can be raised, but I have tried to state broadly both agreements and differences of principle.

I can honestly say that I have not sought to minimize real differences, and yet I think the impression will be that they have been reduced within comparatively small and manageable dimensions. So far as Dr. Moberly and I may be taken as representing opposite antecedents and tendencies, I conceive that we have very nearly come to terms. The outstanding questions between us are not such as to constitute the kind of cleft that many regard as existing in English religion.

It is just this which seems to me to be at the present moment greatly exaggerated. We are told that there is a 'crisis in the Church.' And a crisis no doubt there is for those who desire to make it one, though the quiet citizen who looks round his own neighbourhood will not very often be conscious of it. It is true that the fourth sermon in this volume dealt with a state of things which, compared with what we see around us now, may seem to have receded into a somewhat distant past. I believe that the disturbances to which reference was made would soon have subsided if left to themselves. I seemed, however, to discern a graver symptom in Mr. Walsh's book and in the efforts which were being made to circulate it. Since that time there has been a vigorous muster of hostile forces; and there can be no doubt that at this moment the public mind is seriously agitated both within and without (but more without than within) our own communion. It is the old 'No Popery!' cry, the history of which is sketched on pp. 122–126, raised once more.

It is important that this history should be borne in mind; and still more important that we should each and all go back upon the facts and verify our own impressions of them. The real appeal is to the truth of history. When this appeal is made, I think it becomes clear that the aggressive party does not speak with the voice of the Church of England. It really represents that Puritan element in the Church which, all through the reign of Elizabeth and onwards, did its utmost to force on the English Reformation beyond the point to which it had been carried. These efforts, strenuous as they were, failed. The Elizabethan settlement by no means expelled everything that was Roman; and whatever had a legitimate footing within the Church then must be regarded as having a legitimate footing within it still.

Recent researches by Mr. Frere and Dr. Gee throw a striking light upon this position. The

Marian reaction was evidently drastic, the Elizabethan very much the reverse. The number of clergy deprived in the one was, according to Mr. Frere's cautious estimate, about one in every six (Canon Dixon had put it at one in five); in the other it cannot have been much more than one in forty[1]. In other words, the main body of the clergy in the first part of Elizabeth's reign must have been the same as under Mary, and therefore in antecedents and sympathies Roman. It follows that beliefs and usages not expressly forbidden would be to a large extent in practice continued; and in the absence of such express prohibition I do not see that they can be held to be illegal.

It would be another thing to say that these usages, continued from pre-Reformation times, were all in harmony with the spirit of the English Church. That spirit did not take a definite shape

---

[1] Dr. Gee comes to the conclusion that not many more than two hundred in all were deprived during the first six years of Elizabeth's reign (*The Elizabethan Clergy*, p. 251). As the total number of benefices in the time of Henry VIII is given as 9,285 (Dixon, *History of the Church of England*, iv. 143), to say one in forty would leave a good margin for vacancies, &c.

all at once, but was the result of a process of slow and natural growth. In the course of this certain things were silently cast off; and prolonged disuse may be held to prove that they formed no necessary or integral part of the Anglican system.

This deliberate recession from Roman usage should not be ignored even where it has not issued in positive legislation. And it must be confessed that some recent attempts at revival or imitation have gone beyond the limits of loyalty. But on the other hand, it is well that there should be room for experiment as to what can be assimilated and what cannot. The expansive and many-sided life of the Church in our own day demands breadth and freedom. There are hundreds and thousands of churches in which clergy and people have a complete mutual understanding. In these it may be assumed that spiritual life is finding its natural outlet. Like gravitates towards like; and although perfect adjustments are not to be expected, where substantial agreement exists it should not be disturbed by artificial and external agitation. A generous emulation between different types of religious character and habit is far better for the life of the whole than a frigid uniformity.

Only let us see to it that zeal for the luxuries and refinements of religion is balanced by an equal zeal for what is central and vital. More knowledge, more calm thought about the larger principles of Christianity, and a constant effort to translate these into conduct, are the chief desiderata at present, and the best corrective for absorption in the minutiae of ritual.

Easter, 1899.

PREFACE

TO THE FIRST EDITION

OF the sermons which follow, three were preached before University audiences in the Chapel of Trinity College, Dublin, and at St. Mary's, Oxford, and the fourth in Christ Church Cathedral. Only the first two were preached continuously; the fourth in this volume was third in order of time and fell in the middle of the Long Vacation. I have not hesitated to alter what I had originally written wherever I thought that it could be improved.

There is something that I do not wholly like in preaching upon burning questions. The quiet steady building up of Christian people in permanent truth is without doubt the more excellent way. But it is just the fringe of permanent truth that is apt to be controversial, and it is often through controversy that the solid body of acknowledged truth is enlarged. On the other hand, it is indeed easy for any one to mistake what may seem to him a certain call to express what is in his mind on the topics of the moment. But risks of this sort are risks that must be run. It is impossible to tell how far a call is real until the attempt has been made to respond to it; and attempts that should not have been made very soon find their level and are forgotten.

It has fallen to me in the course of the following pages to speak much and often of a near neighbour and dear friend, to whom, since we were brought together, I have been greatly indebted—and all the more indebted because our antecedents and ways of looking at things are so different. He will not, I know, think it inconsistent with our friendship if I discuss these serious matters with him as freely in public as I should do (if I could) in private. For one who is halting in speech and slow in getting his thoughts into order, the compulsion of print is a distinct advantage. And I have a feeling that the antithesis which subsists between us is one that will need to work itself out on a larger scale, if the reconciliation and concentration of forces for which so many of us are looking is to be accomplished.

During the five or six months which, in the intervals of other things, the preparation of these sermons has covered, events have moved fast in the Church of England, and the situation to-day is not exactly what it was when the sermon which comes last in the volume was preached. The most important fact that has intervened has been the Primate's Charge, which will, I imagine, chiefly be felt as a strong and timely defence of our threatened comprehensiveness. It never was more necessary that this should be maintained, and that in wider interests than our own. The double aspect of our Church constitutes at once its greatest difficulty and its greatest opportunity. If we can overcome the difficulty, and succeed in harmonizing the differences within our own borders, there is a good hope that the effect may be felt beyond them.

Only as this little book was going to press there came into my hands a treatise by the Rev. B. J. Kidd on *The Later Mediaeval Doctrine of the Eucharistic Sacrifice*, published under the auspices of the Church Historical Society. This is a full and exact examination of the subject, and should certainly be consulted by all who desire to see the question touched on p. 87 worked out with detailed precision.

November, 1898.

CONTENTS

I

THE UNITY OF THE CHURCH

I

Now there are diversities of gifts, but the same Spirit. And there are diversities of ministrations, and the same Lord. And there are diversities of workings, but the same God, who worketh all things in all. I COR. xii. 4-6 (R. V.).

THERE are two ways of approaching the New Testament and the institutions and doctrines of the early Church, which stand to each other in rather sharp contrast. One of these has a recognized name and certain recognized canons, but I am not sure that this can be said of the other; and I hesitate to give it a name which might not be accepted and might do it an injustice. The first, of which I think I may speak as recognized, is the Historical Method. The other I may perhaps be allowed, purely for convenience and with all due reserve on the grounds mentioned, to call the Logical Method as opposed to the Historical.

These two methods are related to each other somewhat in the way in which Induction is related to Deduction. I remember that there is, as I suppose the philosophers would tell us, no such thing as pure Induction or pure Deduction ; in every so-called inductive process there is an element of deduction, and in every so-called deductive process there is an element of induction.   But if that is so, the terms would be all the more appropriate as applied to the methods of which I am speaking.   In neither is there anything really hard and fast.   Both are in their way more or less mixed.   Still, very broadly and generally speaking, the tendency of the one may be said to be inductive, and that of the other deductive.   In other words, the tendency of the one is to argue upwards from facts or from particulars to principles, and that of the other is to argue downwards from principles to facts and particulars, and always to interpret the particular in the light of the universal.   The one method, following the course of external events, sees the principle at work gradually emerging from them ; the other, seizes first upon the principle, and with this firmly in hand threads its way through the events, classifying, characterizing, and judging them by their relation to the principle.

For some time past opposite tendencies which

might be thus described, have made themselves
felt in a field of inquiry which is of great
importance in the study of Christian Origins—
the inquiry as to the conception of the Church
in early Christian times and as to the corresponding conception and practical development
of the Ministry. Within the last year they have
been presented probably in clearer antithesis
than ever before—certainly in antithesis so
clear as to bring the question of method into
conscious prominence—by the publication of
two books, the posthumous volume of Dr. Hort's
lectures and sermons entitled *The Christian
Ecclesia* and Dr. Moberly's *Ministerial Priesthood*. Both books stand out above the general
level of current theological literature, the second
perhaps in especial degree because of its very
able dialectic and the uncompromising boldness
and sharpness of outline in which it sets forth
a theory which in recent years, although it has
no doubt been strongly held by a large section
of the Anglican Church, has not in an equal
degree had the ear of the general public.
Perhaps it was time that the balance should
be redressed. In any case it is just through
such sharp formulation of opposing views that

permanent advances in the apprehension of truth are made.

It would be difficult for two writers to adopt more opposite methods. And it seems to me, if I am not mistaken, that this oppositeness of method is answerable for an appearance of greater oppositeness in conclusion than really exists. For the present I take a single point, but that a point which is fundamental in its bearing upon the whole position—'the nature of Church Unity.'

The later writer criticizes the earlier on this head. He finds his conception of the unity of the Church inadequate, and he evidently thinks that the inadequacy is deep rooted, that it goes behind details of exegesis and that it marks an inherent defectiveness of teaching.

There does indeed seem to be a real difference, and one which we certainly ought to look full in the face. But I believe that it is emphasized rather more than it need be emphasized; and so far as I am able to judge it seems to me that the language used by Dr. Hort more exactly represents the tenor of Scripture, and by the careful way in which it is guarded saves us from consequences which we may be glad to be spared.

It is not denied that there is in a great deal of this language the glow of a noble enthusiasm. 'Glow' is the word which best expresses the effect with which this enthusiasm makes its way outwards. Severely self-critical, not ready in expression, and sincere to the remotest fibre of his being, it was impossible for Dr. Hort to set down a syllable of mere rhetoric or that he did not deeply feel. But he was a man of strong convictions; he held nothing on which his mind was really made up that he did not intensely hold; and there cannot be a doubt that this article of his creed was one that he would have himself claimed as a foundation truth of his thinking.

But the purpose with which he wrote was historical. He traces the process by which Church after Church was founded, a process which to the eye of a careless onlooker might have seemed fortuitous; the great Church of Antioch deriving its origin from certain nameless disciples scattered in the persecution which arose about Stephen, visited for a long time by none of the Twelve, and shaping its course in no direct dependence on them, guided and prompted by a little band of prophets and teachers whose names fall rather into the second than the first rank of those which history has handed down to us ; the great Church of Rome even more conspicuously a product in the first instance of what might seem an accidental aggregation of little groups of Christians from this country and from that finding their way as if by a natural magnetism to the centre of the Empire ; the long list of Churches of St. Paul's foundation owning allegiance indeed to him as their founder but owning none to the Churches of Judaea, though at his earnest entreaty using every effort to translate the fellowship of Christians into substantial fact by a liberal contribution to their material needs. A careless onlooker might well, as I have said, see nothing but accident in this. We know that it was not accident, but the working of a Providence never absent from the Church of Christ, but more signally manifest in that age than in any other. The actors in these events, leaders as well as followers, must have been for the time absorbed in them. Only by degrees there would dawn upon their minds the conception of a Church 'one' in the sense of the Nicene Creed, embracing all the scattered

communities in a high transcendental union;
for it was long before there was any such
centralized system of organization as that which
culminated in mediaeval Rome and even then
did not include, or only included imperfectly
and for a short time, the whole of Christendom.
So far as the evidence which has come down
to us permits us to see, St. Paul was the first
to take in the full grandeur of the vision which
these events had been preparing. He gives it
expression for the first time in the Epistle to
the Ephesians. That Epistle is well described
as 'the harmonious outpouring of thoughts that
had long been cherished but had not as yet
found right and profitable opportunity for full
utterance, thoughts that doubtless had grown
and ripened while they lay unspoken, and now
had been kindled afresh by the conjuncture
which had at length been reached in the Divine
ordering of events; for now, after weary years
of struggle and anxiety, what St. Paul recognized
as sure pledges for the essential unity and
essential universality of the Church of Christ
had been visibly bestowed from on high [1].'

Those are Dr. Hort's words; and it would

[1] *The Christian Ecclesia*, p. 280 f.

be easy to quote many others like them which bear the strongest witness that this 'essential unity and essential universality' (i. e. comprehensiveness) of the Church of Christ was very far from being indifferent to him. It did indeed lie very near his heart.

But then he speaks of the unity of the universal Ecclesia as 'a truth of theology and of religion, not a fact of what we call ecclesiastical politics [1].' This is the distinction to which exception is taken [2], or at least to the application of it. It is worth while to note the epithets that are used on the two sides. Dr. Hort, as we have seen, speaks of 'essential unity and essential universality.' On the other side we find the epithets 'dominant,' 'paramount,' 'peremptory' recur several times [3].

I will consider presently the significance and validity of these different modes of expression. But we shall do well first to see how far the opposing views really coincide with each other. For indeed the common ground between them is very large; and that it is so large is, I cannot

---

[1] *The Christian Ecclesia*, p. 168.
[2] *Ministerial Priesthood*, p. 26 f.
[3] Ibid., pp. 3, 9, 10, 26, and perhaps elsewhere.

but think, a cheering and hopeful sign for the extent to which our Church may close its ranks and march forward in the spirit of comradeship to the work that lies before it.

For the purpose of determining the extent of the common ground I will take the analysis of the idea of Church Unity as it is given in the first chapter of *Ministerial Priesthood.* We find there certain lower forms of unity discussed, and not denied or discarded but treated as subservient to the highest.

First there is the idea of what is called a 'purely accidental unity,' as though the Church had consisted in the first instance of a number of individual units which by degrees under pressure of circumstances coalesced into a society. The two authors would be agreed in rejecting this as an adequate account of the origin of the Christian Church, though it might not be an untrue description of certain aspects of the process of unification seen merely from without.

Next is taken up the idea which marks a further step in advance upon this—the idea, namely, that out of such accidental coalescence of units there gradually grew up the conception of unity as an ideal to be aimed at. It is a universal experience that individuals acting in a society are stronger than the same number of individuals acting each alone. And there can be no question that through such practical experience the sense of brotherhood in the smaller Christian communities would be daily strengthened. And from the smaller communities it would pass to the larger groups until these were bound together, in a sort of federation. This too is a *vera causa*, but not a sufficient cause for what we know to have been the course of early Christian History.

Above these lower kinds of unity arising ultimately out of practical advantage rises the philosophical conception based upon the demonstrable incompleteness of the individual life. In connexion with this there occurs the profound remark which is well worth pondering that 'not in abstraction, or isolation, but in communion lies (it may be) the very meaning of personality itself[1].' Man cannot develop the highest part

---

[1] *Ministerial Priesthood*, p. 5. A very similar thought is to be found in Hort, *Hulsean Lectures*, p. 194: 'All life in the higher sense depends on some fellowship, an isolated life is a contradiction in terms. Fellowship is to the higher life what food is to the natural life—without it every power flags and at last perishes.'

of himself except in relation to his fellows.
Thus life in society satisfies a high necessity
or craving of our natures and not merely those
that are lower. The sense of this too no doubt
contributed, however unconsciously, to weld
together the scattered units which made up
the Christian Church.

But for the Christian, supreme above even
this philosophical conception of unity, is the
theological. If the Church is in something
more than mere metaphor the Body of Christ,
if there is circulating through it a continual
flow and return of spiritual forces, derived
directly from Him, if the Spirit which animates
the Body is One, then the Body itself also
must be in essence one. It has its centre not
on earth but in heavenly places, where Christ
sitteth at the right hand of God. It is therefore one in a sense which is truly both essential
and transcendental.

This essential and transcendental unity would
be as fully recognized by Dr. Hort as by his
critic. It is just what he means in speaking
of it as a 'truth of theology or of religion.'
I do not doubt that he would have also
recognized certain consequences which flow

from this. He too would say that this transcendental unity cannot be only transcendental.
It is, and it must be, continually realizing itself
in the Church upon earth. No Christian, and
no society of Christians, can escape the pressing
duty of making the unity which exists in name
more and more real and vital. Let us lay down
all this in the strongest terms possible. But
when we have done so, there will still be two
questions unanswered : (1) the question as to the
extent to which the unity of inward essence
requires a corresponding unity of outward
organization ; (2) the question as to the exact
nature of the obligation which it imposes, the
exact place of this duty in the scale of Christian
duties generally.

(1) Unity is one thing, uniformity is another.
A high degree of 'essential' unity is compatible
with a much lower degree of formal unity.
When we are considering the unity of the
Church, the most obvious analogy that presents
itself is that of the unity of the State. But in
the case of the State the unity of the body
politic is not only consistent with, but it actually
gains from a great amount of local variety.

Take the British Empire at this moment. Is

it the less a unit, is it the less an empire because it includes within its bounds a perplexing
multiplicity of local constitutions—vassal states,
protected states, crown colonies, self-governing
colonies? Experience has taught us as a nation
that different races and communities of different
history and origin are not all to be governed
upon the same lines. It has taught us that
a loose tie may be far more effective than one
that seems closer. It has taught us the wisdom
of allowing constitutions to grow and adapt
themselves to varying needs and circumstances.
It has taught us the strength and flexibility that
comes from a generous recognition of local
freedom. The impressive celebrations of last
year, with the spirit of loyalty which they evoked
and the deep-seated strength to which they bore
witness, put the seal for ever upon a lesson
which had been slowly learnt.

Something of the same lesson had been learnt
centuries ago by a race with no less practical
instincts than our own. The pages of the New
Testament are studded with indications of the
way in which imperial Rome knew how to build
up a like unity upon diversity. The politarchs
at Thessalonica, the *duumviri* with their lictors

at Philippi, the Asiarchs at Ephesus, the legatus
in Syria, the procurator in Judaea, the pro-
consuls in Cyprus and at Corinth, the tetrarchs
of Galilee and Ituraea, the two Agrippas with
their title of King, remind us how many and
varied types of government and administration
were held to be, and were, entirely compatible
with inner cohesion and stability.

I do not quote these examples to prove at
once that a like degree of variety is admissible
in the case of the Church. I only quote them
as evidence that a stringent conclusion cannot
be drawn *a priori*. It does not follow that
because the Church is one, it can have but
a single type of outward organization. What
types it can have, and what type it is best that
it should have, must be determined by other
methods, and in particular by the old appeal to
Scripture and to History.

(2) To the Scriptures also we must go if we
would determine the nature of the obligation
entailed by the unity of the Church. We have
seen that this has been described on the one
hand by such terms as 'dominant,' 'paramount,'
'peremptory,' taking it at once into the region
of practice and giving to it a foremost place in

the complex scheme of Christian duties; and on the other hand we had it described as rather a 'truth of theology and religion' than a fact of ecclesiastical politics.

To which of these two descriptions does the language of the New Testament correspond most nearly? Unity of spirit, harmoniousness of action, mutual deference and consideration, the absence of self-assertion, are no doubt enjoined in the imperative mood. That the Church as the Body of Christ is one is a postulate of Christian belief[1]. But as this oneness is conditioned by the presence of the Holy Spirit, it would seem that wherever there were the fruits of the Spirit the oneness in question was in some measure satisfied. Not a word is said about uniformity of outward organization. And the great passage in which the Lord Himself speaks most directly of the oneness of His followers, is not a command having reference to the present but a prayer pointing to a distant future. 'Neither for these only do I pray, but for them also that believe on Me through their word; that they may all be one; even as Thou, Father, art in Me, and I in Thee, that they also

[1] Eph. iv. 4.

may be in Us : that the world may believe that
Thou didst send Me. And the glory which
Thou hast given Me I have given unto them ;
that they may be one, even as We are one ;
I in them, and Thou in Me, that they may be
perfected into one ; that the world may know
that Thou didst send Me, and lovedst them, even
as Thou lovedst Me[1].' There is nothing here
that we can call 'peremptory'; the unity of
Christians is not treated as a matter of command, written as it were on tables of stone, but
as a principle working its way gradually to
fulfilment under that Divine Providence which
governs the world. Our Lord prays for this
fulfilment in the same manner in which He
bids us pray that the Kingdom of God may
come, and that His will may be done on earth
as it is in heaven.

These distinctions will seem to some fine-
drawn, but their practical importance is seen
when we come to apply them to the actual state
of things around us.

We are confronted with the fact that the
unity of the Church has been broken. Christendom is divided into a number of bodies, many

[1] John xvii. 20-23.

of which do not recognize or hold communion with each other. Some are further removed from organic unity than others. And the judgement which we form of these separated bodies will depend directly upon what we take to be the nature of the unity of the Church, and the nature also of the obligation to maintain it. On the view which we form of these points will hang our estimate, not only of the fault incurred in the breach of unity, but also of the possibilities of reunion.

Our great divisions date mainly from the sixteenth century. And it is very probably true that throughout that century there was an insufficient sense of the obligation of unity. From that time to this, especially throughout Northern Europe, the centrifugal tendency—if we may call it so—has prevailed. At the present moment there is a reaction, and men are earnestly seeking to reunite the severed members.

Of course there were reasons for the severance. And it is just here that the question as to the nature of the obligation of unity comes in, where one obligation is weighed against another, and where the lower has to yield to the higher.

As a problem of history the estimate which we form of the Reformation is most delicate and difficult. It greatly needs renewed examination with full knowledge of the facts, and with more resolute impartiality of judgement.

I can only speak as one who does his best to aim at the latter qualification. My own more special studies have lain too much in other directions for me to make any claim to the former.

At its best the Reformation was a moral revolt against corruptions and abuses which had reached a climax at the moment when it broke out. It was an intellectual revolt in defence of nascent truth which it was sought to suppress, as well as against perverted developments which could not stand the test of reason. It was a spiritual revolt against doctrines which at least in their popular acceptation were too often and too grossly materialized.

If we are to do justice to the leaders of the Reformation we must bear these things in mind. We must give them full credit for the better part of the motives which impelled them to undertake the conflict, and for the courage and steadfastness with which it was sustained. We must remember what the conflict meant, a very different thing from sitting in our easy chairs and writing to the newspapers as we do to-day. We must remember also how difficult it was for men in all the confusion and heat of battle to see the exact perspective of things as we may now hope to see it.

But, on the other hand, if we would do justice to the forces which made for resistance, we shall have at every turn to check the facts as to the extent of the corruptions and abuses—or, to put the same thing more positively, as to the amount of genuine and sincere Christianity which existed along with and in spite of them. I feel sure that Protestant writers have too much underrated this[1]. We shall have to distinguish between the popular distortions of doctrine and practice and the same doctrine and practice under a more enlightened interpretation.

[1] Let us, e. g., put before our minds one or two facts : that the *Imitation* was a product of the century before the Reformation, and that the conditions under which it was produced had a rather wide extension ; that it was in the same century that Fra Angelico was painting in his cell at St. Mark's ; that Luther himself derived a great part of his impulse to the spiritual life from Staupitz and the Augustinians ; that Sir Thomas More died for conscience sake and for his fidelity to the old order—the whole Reformation produced no finer character.

Among the points which we should have to consider is one which has lately been brought up afresh, and which affects intimately the whole course of controversy both in those days and in our own. This is the relation of the inward to the outward, of the forms and institutions in which the religion of the time was embodied to the religion itself. In the controversies of the Reformation much stress was laid upon the antithesis of inward and outward, and stress is continually being laid upon it by the advocates of Reformed teaching. In particular it played a prominent part in Bishop Lightfoot's well-known Essay on the Christian Ministry.

This position of Bishop Lightfoot's is challenged by Dr. Moberly, who insists that it is wrong to put the outward into antithesis to the inward. The outward, it is maintained, should be rather the natural expression of the inward. The complex system of the Christian ministry and Christian ordinances should be the appropriate vehicle of the life within. If we look out into the world of nature we see everywhere body in the closest relation to spirit. 'All flesh is not the same flesh: but there is one flesh of men, and another flesh of beasts, and another flesh of birds, and another of fishes[1].' The law holds good that the inner vital force clothes itself with a corresponding organism. And this organism becomes as necessary to the life for which it is the vehicle as the life is necessary to it.

We must needs regard this as a sound analogy, and we must accept the warning which goes along with it. If there is a serious divergence between the outward and the inward,—if the outward becomes utterly inadequate or faulty as a vehicle of the inward, the proper remedy is to correct the outward, not to destroy or ignore it; to re-establish the missing harmony, not to despair of producing any harmony at all.

The reminder which we have received of these truths is well-timed. It is to be hoped that we shall not forget them.

And yet after all is there not great excuse for those who have pressed the contrast between inward and outward too sharply? May they not seem to have the highest authority at least for the intention of what they do? The feeling of contrast between inward and outward is with-

[1] 1 Cor. xv. 39.

out doubt very widespread, especially on all the Protestant side of Christendom.　And when we inquire after its origin I strongly suspect that it is due, ultimately if not immediately, more than to any other cause, to the general impression left by the reading of the Gospels.　The reading may be to some extent a misreading, an imperfect reading, a reading which does not sufficiently note the whole of the context ; still the mistake is not unnatural.　The minds of Christians have been haunted all through the centuries by those scathing denunciations of the Scribes and Pharisees, the religious leaders of the day.　'Woe unto you, scribes and Pharisees, hypocrites! for ye tithe mint and anise and cummin, and have left undone the weightier matters of the law, judgement, and mercy, and faith : but these ye ought to have done, and not to have left the other undone. . . . Woe unto you, scribes and Pharisees, hypocrites! for ye cleanse the outside of the cup and of the platter, but within they are full from extortion and excess (i.e. the cup and the platter are filled with the proceeds of extortion and licence, ill-gotten gains and the material of self-indulgence).　Thou blind Pharisee, cleanse first the inside of the cup and of the platter, that the outside thereof may become clean also[1].'

When we look into such passages carefully, we see how exquisitely they are balanced,— just the right amount of stress, neither less nor more: 'These ye ought to have done, and not to have left the other undone. . . . cleanse first the inside of the cup and of the platter, that the outside thereof may become clean also.' The tithing of mint and anise and cummin is not to be neglected. The greater duty does not cancel the less. And the cleansing of the inside of the cup has for part of its object that the outside may be clean. The words of grace do indeed need careful and accurate study if we are to obey the maxim to 'see life steadily and see it whole'—not merely to discern the right from the wrong, but to observe a due balance and proportion in the discriminating of right and wrong.

And yet, human nature being what it is, so hasty and so impulsive, so impatient of study and so prone to take sides and see one thing in glaring light and another not at all, can we be surprised if hundreds and thousands and

[1] Matt. xxiii. 23-26.

tens of thousands of Christians have risen from the perusal of this twenty-third chapter of St. Matthew with the belief that the external and official embodiment of religion is in constant danger of corruption, and that it is more likely to contradict than to represent the motions of the Spirit within?

If it were not for the injustice of arguing simply from one age to another, we should have to confess that the Gospels do go a long way in the support of such a paradox. 'Thou, when thou fastest, anoint thy head, and wash thy face; that thou be not seen of men to fast, but of thy Father which is in secret[1].' Here we have an extreme case. The lower law that a certain attitude of mind finds its expression in a certain practice is not only suspended but reversed by the action of a higher law which imperiously demands sincerity and singleness of motive. And wherever there is a like collision of principle the Gospel rule leaves us in no manner of doubt which we ought to follow. There are other requirements of the Gospel which are more dominant, more paramount, more peremptory than the requirement of external unity or

[1] Matt. vi. 17 f.

the maintenance of traditional forms of eccle- /
siastical or liturgical order.

If, therefore, the Reformers went to greater
lengths than they need have done,—if they
considered too little (as I believe they did
consider) the obligation of a full and real unity
among Christians, not only in the sense and
spirit of brotherhood, but in the outward forms
of an organization expressive of brotherhood,
we must at least give them credit for setting
the greater commandments of the law in their
proper place. If they broke up the unity—
not, be it remembered, of the whole Church
but of the Western Church, for the separation
of East and West had taken place centuries
before and on grounds still more inadequate
—they aroused themselves to do this in deference to what seemed to them the yet more
imperative claims of right and truth. We need
not think that their right was perfect right or their
truth the whole truth and nothing but the truth,
to regard them as having a considerable degree
of justification for their action, so much justification as should in any case exempt them from
excessive blame. They had the root of the
matter. They had the earnest desire to do

what was right and to believe what was true; and in pursuit of this end they were ready to sacrifice their personal ease, to run great risks, and even to put in jeopardy life itself.

And another thing that needs to be remembered is that none of the Reformers believed them-selves to be breaking the true unity of the Church. There was not one who would not have confessed from his heart that the Church is one. Some of them, it is true, like Zwingli and Calvin, sought this unity in the invisible Church rather than in the visible. And for the stress which they laid upon this distinction the crying faults of the visible Church must bear a great part of the blame.

But others like Luther and Melanchthon, though they make the distinction, do not press it to the extent of antithesis or contrast but see that the visible and the invisible Church are really the same. The teaching of the Reformers on this head is very interesting and deserves to be set out in some detail. Those who desire to look into the subject will find this ably done in one of the collected essays[1] of Albrecht Ritschl.

[1] *Gesammelte Aufsätze*, Freiburg i. B. und Leipzig, 1893.

Time prevents me from tracing as I should like to do the course of the doctrine in Huss and Zwingli. And in regard to Calvin I can only pause to point out that even he allows that 'wherever we see the word of God sincerely preached and sincerely heard, where we see the Sacraments administered according to Christ's ordinance, there it can in no wise be doubted that there is in some sense a Church of God (*illic aliquam esse dei ecclesiam nullo modo ambigendum est*)[1].' These are almost the familiar words of our own Nineteenth Article, and they are valuable as far as they go, though not carried out quite consistently.

Luther goes a step further. He distinguishes indeed the Spiritual Church, the object of faith, which he identifies with the 'Communion of Saints,' and the 'Corporeal Church,' the outward marks of which are, not Rome or any other local centre, but Baptism, Sacrament, and Gospel. It is true that he speaks somewhat disparagingly of this hierarchical corporeal Church as in its quality as corporeal, in its hierarchy and its ritual, an ordinance of men; but though he gives them different names he

[1] *Inst.* iv. i. par. 9.

regards them as really only different aspects of
the same Church. 'The first,' he says, 'which
is natural, thorough, essential, and real, we will
call a spiritual inward Christendom. The other
which is artificial and external, we will call
a bodily and outward Christendom, not,' he
goes on, 'that we desire to separate them but
(to keep them) together, as though I were to
speak of a man and were to call him on the
side of his soul a spiritual man and on
the side of his body a bodily[1].' And this
language is made yet more explicit by Melanchthon who will not hear of an invisible Church
apart from the visible. 'And let us not invent,'
he says, 'a Church invisible and without voice
(*invisibilem et mutam*), though consisting of men
alive in the flesh, but let the eyes as well as
the mind contemplate the multitude of them
that are called, i. e. of those who profess the
Gospel of God[2].'

I quote these passages because they present
a welcome coincidence, from a perhaps rather
unexpected quarter, with a leading idea of
Dr. Moberly's who insists that 'the Church

[1] *Werke*, xviii. 1215, *ap.* Ritschl, *u. s.*, p. 76.
[2] *Corp. Ref.* xxi. 825, *ap.* Ritschl, p. 86.

militant and the kingdom triumphant are the same Church,' and who illustrates their identity by the continuous personality of the individual saint— the saint on earth with all his sins and short-comings, and the same saint in heaven purified and glorified.

It will be said that even if an agreement is reached on this head—as I think it may be reached—the main difficulty is still left, viz. the difficulty as to what we are to say of those good men outside the pale whom we cannot think that God will reject, even though they have not complied and perhaps have not had the opportunity of complying with all the con-ditions of membership of the Visible Church. But is not the answer something of this kind ?

Theology is meant for normal conditions, not for abnormal. We trouble ourselves too much about these latter, which we can in fact only leave to God—assured that in so doing we are leaving them to One who knoweth whereof we are made and remembereth that we are but dust, to One who will make every allowance that can possibly be made for the errors as well as for the misfortunes of His children.

And for the rest it seems to me that in this as in many other controversies which divide men most at the present time, the issue is very largely one of words rather than of things. Those who insist on the Invisible Church mean by the Church not the society of the potentially redeemed, but of the actually and ultimately redeemed, the congregation of the 'just made perfect.' Those who lay stress on the Visible Church mean by the Church the society of those who bear certain outward marks of being Christ's people. There can be no question that both these are real entities, but they are also very different entities; the common name of 'Church' includes them both; and it constantly happens that one set of persons in speaking of the Church has the one idea in their minds, while another set of persons in using the same comprehensive title has the other. Nor are even these two senses exhaustive. The 'Ideal Church,' though it covers in part what was aimed at by the phrase 'Invisible Church,' is not identical with it, and it stands in a different relation to the outward society as we see it. Here again when we speak of the Church some may be thinking of the Catholic Church, the Church Universal (of which in its turn the definitions may be different), some of the National Church, some even of the simple congregation.

Now if in every case in which debate arises about the Church the disputants were careful to add the discriminating epithet which showed precisely which of the divergent senses they had in view, their meaning would be clear, and the rest of the world would know against what and for what they were arguing. But this careful definition of terms is usually wanting. And the consequence is infinite confusion, and a vague interchange of random strokes which wound those for whom they were not intended.

'If there is battle, 'tis battle by night, we stand in the darkness, Here in the mêlée of men, Ionian and Dorian on both sides, Signal and password known ; which is friend and which is foeman [1] ? '

This is one aspect of things, the aspect which is depressing and discouraging. But there is of necessity another aspect which is more hopeful. If so much of our present contro-

[1] Clough, *Bothie*, canto ix.

D

versies turns upon false issues,—if we see
men upon all sides using different language
because they are thinking about different things,
attacking others for what they do not hold and
holding themselves other views than those
which their opponents attribute to them, ought
it not to be possible, by carefully correcting
our ideas from the outset, by ascertaining
exactly what our opponents mean as well as
what we mean ourselves, by looking throughout
less at words and names than at realities, to
find a much larger amount of common ground
than we have done hitherto, and to mitigate the
bitterness of conflict by removing all that is
removable of its causes? I firmly believe that
it is possible to do this. The moment may
seem inauspicious, when the minds of men
are heated and the air is full of tumult. But
that is all the more urgent reason why the
friends of peace on both sides should lay
their thoughts calmly before each other and
seek to bring them into closer harmony.

II

THE ORIGIN OF THE MINISTRY

D 2

II

And God hath set some in the Church, first apostles, secondly prophets, thirdly teachers, then miracles, then gifts of healings, helps, governments [wise counsels, R. V. marg.], divers kinds of tongues. I COR. xii. 28.

ARE we to conceive of the Christian Ministry as originating by devolution from above, or by evolution from below? The question has recently been propounded to us in a very trenchant manner, and it has received a very trenchant answer. But as this answer is given in the form of a criticism of one, if not two, of our most illustrious scholars, the two theories may be regarded as directly confronting each other, and it is highly desirable that they should be examined, and that the decision between them should be made as deliberately and carefully as possible.

The question may be approached in several different ways, and by different methods. The

particular method which I propose to myself will
be that of following the history of the Ministry
in its earlier stages, and at each step in the
process endeavouring to determine which of
the two theories fits the data most satisfactorily.
We must be prepared for the possibility that
there may be elements of truth in both, and if
that should be the case, we shall try to discover
what they are and how they are to be combined.

There are two points which appear to need
a little clearing up at the outset. When we
speak of devolution and of evolution as applied
to the Ministry we may mean one of two things.
We may have in our minds the commission to
minister in the holders of office, or we may
be thinking not so much of the holders of office
as of the offices themselves as they emerge in
history.

Bishop Lightfoot's sketch of the growth of
the Christian Ministry no doubt has reference
mainly to the latter. But the criticism which
is directed against him appears to embrace
both at once. It may be right that it should
do this; it may be true that the one question
involves the other. But it may conduce to
clearness of thought if in our minds we keep

them apart. This, for instance, is the way in which the problem is stated. 'Must true ministerial "character" be in all cases conferred from above ? Or may it sometimes, and with equal validity, be evolved from below ? Is uninterrupted transmission from those who had the power to transmit a real essential ? or can the Church originate, at any point, a new ministry whose commission of authority should exceed or transcend what had been ministerially received[1].' I submit that however they may be connected, the transmission of ministerial 'character' or commission and the creating of a new form of ministry are not quite the same thing. And when Bishop Lightfoot is criticized for ignoring the whole question, I should have thought that what he really did was to try to consider the second half without considering the first. I am not clear that he was wrong in this. In other words: the question whether the Church did or did not create a new form of ministry seems to be a question of historical fact which can be answered as such, and, if it can, ought to be so answered independently of any further principle which may be involved

---

[1] *Ministerial Priesthood*, p. 116.

in it. I propose myself to take the two propositions in this order. How far this can be
done legitimately should appear from time to
time on the particular issues.

Another preliminary question on which it is
well to have an understanding is as to what
is meant by evolution in such a connexion as
that before us. There is no doubt a mechanical
and godless theory of evolution which would
be repudiated by the Christian scholars who
have dealt with the Ministry. For them, so
far as they have ever used the word or so far
as it can fairly be used to describe their views,
it is as far as possible from being either mechanical or godless. What a Christian means
by 'evolution' is only a particular method, and as
it would seem the usual method of the Divine
working. Behind it, in it, through it there is
always the Providence of God, shaping the
course of human events in accordance with His
sovereign Will. If the God of Israel, watching
over His people, slumbered not nor slept, as
little can we think of the Author of the New
Covenant as slumbering or sleeping. If that
New Covenant was to be conveyed throughout
the world, we may well see His hand in every

step which conduced to its more efficient propagation.

One part of the Divine working may help to illustrate another. There is nothing in which we believe the Spirit of God to have been more immediately present than in the process of Revelation. Yet God's revelation of Himself as we see it is made to us through men. And these men, prophets or 'wise men' or apostles, or whatever they may be, did not by becoming the vehicles of it lose any of their attributes as men. They wrote down naturally what they thought, and their thoughts have an inner coherence with which the Divine action upon them does not interfere, though the result, when we see it, is not what would have been attained by any unaided natural process. We may take a verse in 1 Thessalonians as a typical description: 'For this cause we also thank God without ceasing, that, when ye received from us the word of the message, even the word of God, ye accepted it not as the word of men, but, as it is in truth, the word of God, which also worketh in you that believe[1].' The preaching of St. Paul was a genuine human product and

[1] 1 Thess. ii. 13.

expression of the mind of the Apostle, but it was not one whit the less the word of God speaking through him. And precisely in the same way we may be prepared to find the forms of Christian Ministry growing, as it might seem, out of ordinary human needs, 'the creation of successive experiences, and changes of circumstance,' and yet all the time carrying out a Divine plan in a Divinely appointed way. When we speak of 'evolution' let it be this which we are understood to mean.

An inquiry as to the history of the Ministry naturally begins with the Apostles. And here we find ourselves in a region which has of late been the scene of somewhat sharp debate. Is it the case that the Apostles (i. e. the Twelve) received 'a formal commission of authority for government from Christ Himself[1]'?

We are apt to think of the Twelve as if the title 'Apostle' were far more freely given them in the Gospels than it is, and as if they were from the first invested with powers of which there is no trace. The name appears to have been given them with a very definite significance.

---

[1] Hort, *Christian Ecclesia*, p. 84; cf. Moberly, *Ministerial Priesthood*, p. 29; Gore, *Ep. to the Ephesians*, p. 269 ff.

We are told that our Lord appointed Twelve, to whom He gave this name, 'that they might be with Him, and that He might send them forth (ἵνα ἀποστέλλῃ αὐτούς) to preach, and to have authority (ἐξουσίαν) to cast out demons[1].' The word indeed appears to have its proper sense of 'missioner.' Their nearness to the person of Jesus seemed to have for its object in the first instance to fit them for their 'mission.' During their Master's lifetime this mission of theirs appears to have been a small and subordinate matter, of less importance in itself than as a prelude or preliminary exercise for their great commission in the future. It was not until their Lord was on the point of departure that the greater commission to 'go and make disciples of all the nations[2]' was unfolded to them.

Suspending for the moment our judgement upon a group of sayings in the Gospels, I think it may be said that there is nothing else in the Gospels and Acts which might not be sufficiently accounted for as the Providential outgrowth of this position. It was inevitable that those who had stood so near the person

[1] Mark iii. 14 f.   [2] Matt. xxviii. 19.

of the Lord, who were supposed to know His mind, and who were able to tell so much more than any one else about Him, should take the lead, or have it willingly conceded to them. We find the function of the Apostles as witnesses to Christ, and in particular to His Resurrection strongly insisted upon. And for the rest as they had been the most prominent of our Lord's disciples during His life, so also were they the most prominent after His Ascension. It is in keeping with the view that the deference paid to them was natural and spontaneous that just those come to the front who possessed a natural ascendency of character, while the rest remain, so far as our evidence goes, very much in the background. It should be remembered also that St. James, 'the Lord's brother,' whatever the precise nature of his authority, probably did not derive it from the fact that he had had a place among the Twelve.

We are expressly told that the action taken as a result of the Conference at Jerusalem was that of 'the Apostles and the elders with the whole Church[1].' It is surely a straining of

[1] Acts xv. 22. It cannot be called strict exegesis to say with Canon Gore that the passage (Acts xv. 24–28) implied 'a govern-

the text to see in this any special prerogative of the Apostles. They act as leaders of the Church and give shape to its resolutions, but those resolutions go forth with the authority of the Church as a whole. The letter which is addressed to the Gentile Christians of Antioch and the surrounding district is written in the names of the Apostles and presbyters, but the express mention of the presbyters shows that the Apostles are not acting by themselves, and the fact that the presbyters of the Church of Jerusalem could have as such no authority whatever over the Church of Antioch may be taken as proof that Apostles and presbyters together are really writing in their representative capacity. Behind them they have the assembly of the whole Church. We observe further that the conditions as to the intercourse of Jews with Gentiles laid down in the letter, although there is claimed for them the sanction of the Holy Ghost,—although, that is, there was an evident consciousness that the meeting of which the letter was the outcome was moved by that prophetic inspiration with which so many of

mental authority, which, if it is shared by the presbyters, is substantially that of the Apostles' (*Ep. to Eph.*, p. 270).

its members were endowed, and although the conditions in question are thus imposed by a weight of authority greater than that of any recorded act since the Day of Pentecost, yet rapidly fell into desuetude and were dropped simply because the course of events left them behind and without any formal abrogation. In this they supply a warning that the Providence of God works far more by the active teaching of history than by any processes of formal authentication.

The history of the Church of Antioch generally points the same moral. It is a Church with which so far as we can see—and in this case the argument from silence seems valid— Apostles *qua* Apostles appear to have had extremely little to do. It was founded without their aid. When it has existed for some time they send Barnabas, but only to report. He reports and exhorts, but nothing more. We hear much of 'prophets' in connexion with it— not only of the little group which send forth Paul and Barnabas on their mission, but also Agabus and Judas and Silas. There can be no doubt that the life of the Spirit was strong within the Church, and yet we hear nothing of

any formal organization. When relief is to
be sent to the Churches of Judaea those who
send it are described simply as 'the disciples[1].'
When Paul and Barnabas are sent up to attend
the Conference the word used is ἔταξαν, without
subject expressed. The letter in reply is addressed simply to 'the brethren in Antioch[2],'
&c., and the same term is used twice in the
following context along with[3] τὸ πλῆθος as descriptive of the Church. Is this accident? We
cannot be sure that it is not. No doubt the
Church at Antioch received an organization
similar to that of the other Churches sooner
or later, but the time seems to have been
delayed.

So far as we have gone we have seen nothing
to require or even to suggest that the Apostles
were invested with any specific authority, other
than that which must naturally and inevitably
(i.e. Providentially) have attached to them. But
we have left behind certain passages in the
Gospels to which it will now be well to return.
They are first the promise to St. Peter that
to him should be given the keys of the kingdom
of heaven, and that what he bound on earth

---

[1] Acts xi. 29.   [2] Ibid. xv. 23.   [3] Ibid. vv. 30, 32, 33.

should be bound in heaven, and what he loosed
on earth should be loosed in heaven [1]. Then
a similar promise to the whole body [2]; the subject
previously mentioned is 'the disciples,' which
is ambiguous. And lastly we have St. John's
account of the meeting in the upper room
on the evening of the first Easter Day, when
the risen Lord breathes upon those who are
assembled, there, saying 'Receive ye the Holy
Ghost: whose soever sins ye forgive, they are
forgiven unto them; whose soever sins ye retain,
they are retained [3].'

In these passages there is no doubt a distinct
committal of powers, in the one case, as it would
seem, of framing laws or deciding what was
binding and what was not; in the other case of
declaring the conditions of forgiveness, whether
(as Bishop Westcott holds) for classes or for
individuals. On whom are these powers conferred? In the first instance the recipient is
without doubt St. Peter in his single person,
perhaps as to some extent representative, but
how far is not defined. In the second passage
'the disciples' *may* mean, but do not certainly

---

[1] Matt. xvi. 19.   [2] Ibid. xviii. 18.   [3] John xx. 22 f.

mean the Twelve. In the third passage it is
a debated point who were addressed. If we
take the narrative in St. Luke to supplement
that in St. John those present are 'the Eleven'
and those who were with them, that is the
nucleus of the Church of Jerusalem. Just
before the appearance of the Lord the two way-
farers who had returned from Emmaus were
added to the number. If it was the same upper
room in which we find the disciples met in
Acts i, there would be an additional presumption that the gathering was not confined to the
Apostles.

It cannot be said that any one of these
passages points to powers conferred upon the
Twelve, as such. It is more probable than
not that others were included in the commission
given besides the Twelve. And even if the
Twelve had a certain prerogative, it would seem
to be less in their own right than as representing the whole body of the Church.

There is another group of passages in which
the Apostles are singled out more expressly.
I refer in a lower degree to the place in
Ephesians where the Church is described as
'built upon the foundation of the apostles and

prophets [1]'—where the way in which 'prophets' (i. e. probably the New Testament prophets) are coupled with the Apostles takes away somewhat from the exceptional position assigned to the latter; moreover it is sufficiently clear that the term 'Apostles' is used in the wider sense as in 1 Cor. xii. 28, Eph. iv. 11, and the *Didaché*, and is not confined to the Twelve. The Twelve are really in view in Matt. xix. 28, where it is said that the twelve Apostles shall sit on twelve thrones, judging the twelve tribes of Israel, and in Rev. xxi. 14, where the wall of the heavenly city is described as having 'twelve foundations, and on them twelve names of the twelve apostles of the Lamb.' The sacred number 'twelve' was deeply fixed among the religious associations of Israel; τὸ δωδεκάφυλον[2] repre-sents the Chosen People as an ideal unit; and St. James, writing as a Christian, addresses his epistle to the 'twelve tribes' in a similar ideal sense. No doubt these allusions imply a special dignity on the part of the Twelve, but there is nothing to show that this dignity included a direct commission to govern. The nearest ana-logue would be that of the Patriarchs. The Jew

[1] Eph. ii. 20.   [2] Acts xxvi. 7.

looked back wistfully to his descent from the Patriarchs[1], and the Christian in like manner traced his spiritual descent to the Twelve Apostles; but in neither case is the precedence involved other than one of honour.

The case of St. Paul illustrates well the process by which a position of honour became also one of authority; but it does not carry the argument further than this. The apostleship of St. Paul had about it something irregular as compared with that of the Twelve. He cannot quite strictly be regarded as incorporated in their number. The three places where he speaks of his 'apostleship'[2] all seem to have the missionary character strongly impressed upon them. The 'seal' of his apostleship to which he points most triumphantly consists in the converts he has made, the Churches he has founded. The proof of it which the Judaean apostles accepted was the actual success of his missionary labours. Even if we could suppose that St. Paul succeeded to any express prerogative conferred upon the Twelve, I should still think that the authority which he exercised

[1] ὧν οἱ πατέρες Rom. ix. 5; cf. iv. 1, xi. 28 f., &c.
[2] Rom. i. 5; 1 Cor. ix. 2; Gal. ii. 8.

turned far less on this than on his claims as
the founder or spiritual 'father' of his Churches,
on his force and ascendency of character, and
on the gifts of the Spirit with which he was
richly endowed. I doubt if the Epistles contain
anything which will not be found to fall under
one or other of these heads.

It were much to be wished that we knew more
about the wider use of the name 'apostle'—its
use I mean not merely for the 'delegate' of
a particular Church, as in 2 Cor. viii. 23, but
for what would seem to be a lesser copy of
the original institution. Suspected before, as
e. g. by Bishop Lightfoot, this use has been
proved beyond dispute by the discovery of the
Didaché, in which the wandering apostle and the
wandering prophet clearly take precedence of
the officers of the local Church. The existence
of this wider sense creates a certain amount of
ambiguity in more than one passage. It would
be a pertinent question to ask how far the
peculiar claim which is made for the Twelve
is supposed to extend. If it includes St. Paul,
does it also include St. Barnabas and St. James,
the Lord's brother? If it includes these, does
it include the whole class referred to in the

Didaché? And if it includes the whole class, on what ground is the claim made for those outside the direct recipients of the two commissions given by our Lord before and after His Resurrection? The absence of any sharp boundary between the Twelve and the larger class who bore the same name involves the exclusive claim which is made for the Twelve in serious difficulties.

After the Twelve the next appointment of which we read in the New Testament is that of the Seven, in whom we shall probably not be wrong in seeing the prototypes of the later order of ' Deacons.' The account of this appointment is so instructive that I shall venture to read it as it stands. ' Now in these days, when the number of the disciples was multiplying, there arose a murmuring of the Grecian Jews [Hellenists] against the Hebrews, because their widows were neglected in the daily ministration. And the twelve called the multitude of the disciples unto them, and said, It is not fit that we should forsake the word of God, and serve tables. Look ye out therefore, brethren, from among you seven men of good report, full of the Spirit and of wisdom, whom we may appoint over

this business. But we will continue stedfastly
in prayer, and in the ministry of the word. . . .
And they chose—seven whose names are given—
whom they set before the apostles: and when they
had prayed, they laid their hands on them [1].'

May I say that the view which I am taking
of the origin of the Christian Ministry as a
whole might be regarded as modelled upon this
passage? It includes both the principles of
evolution and of devolution. It is indeed an
exact example of what I understand by 'evolution.' The appointment of the Seven arises out
of what might be called ordinary natural causes,
which because they are so described may none
the less be carrying out a larger Divine purpose.
In proposing the appointment the Twelve are
moved by considerations of the higher expe-
diency. The initiative comes from them, and
certain parts of the formal appointment are
discharged by them—whether claimed by them
as a right or spontaneously left to them by
the Church, does not appear. The Church as
a whole also takes an active part. They give
a willing consent to the proposal. They select
the candidates, examine their qualifications, and

[1] Acts vi. 1–6.

present them for the laying on of hands. One can almost see by such a passage how easily and naturally practical questions might solve themselves, without any formal constitution or established rule—by spontaneous deference and good feeling on the one side, and desire for the public good and the enlisting of willing service on the other. The distribution of parts is perfectly appropriate, and would be equally appropriate whether there were any formal commission behind it or not. The proof of such a commission appears to me very imperfect. But even if it existed, I would far rather lay stress on the beautiful spirit of co-operation which runs through the narrative. The ideal temper, the truly Christian temper, the temper befitting the followers of Him who bade His disciples not to let themselves be called Rabbi, seems to be such as this,—where there is no raising of the question of authority, where it is neither asserted on the one hand nor denied on the other, where it is not even felt with any touch of self consciousness on either side, but where there is just a quiet, affectionate deference, which has no laws because it needs none.

This may be the point at which a few words

should be said on the much debated question
of the 'laying on of hands.' It was used at
what we should call 'Ordinations' or the solemn
setting apart for office, but it is not simply to
be identified with this. It accompanied any act
of blessing, as we see by many examples, from
the blessing of Ephraim and Manasseh by
Jacob to the children whom our Lord took
up in His arms, 'laying His hands upon them[1].'
A similar act was frequently employed by our
Lord in His miracles of healing[2], and by others,
as by Ananias in restoring St. Paul to sight[3], and
by St. Paul himself in the healing of Publius[4].
Nor in the cases of consecration was it confined
to consecration to office. The 'prophets and
teachers,' we read, laid their hands upon Paul
and Barnabas, when they were sent out on
their new work of carrying the Gospel to the
Gentiles[5]. The same passage shows that although Philip the Evangelist did not himself
'lay hands' upon his Samaritan converts, but
waited for the coming of Peter and John, the
rite was not reserved solely for Apostles, as

---

[1] Mark x. 16 ; Matt. xix. 15.
[2] Mark vi. 5 ; cf. i. 41, v. 23, &c.   [3] Acts ix. 12, 17.
[4] Ibid. xxviii. 8.   [5] Ibid. xiii. 3.

indeed we find it in the case of Timothy also administered by the whole presbytery[1].

These varied uses at the same time make it clear that although employed (as blessing was employed) naturally and preferably by a superior, the act did not denote the transmission of a power or energy from one who had it to one who had it not, because this would not apply either to the case of Ananias or to the prophets and teachers at Antioch sending Paul and Barnabas on a mission which was wholly new. It seems to have been rather a symbolical act, in its origin similar to the symbolical acts of the prophets of the Old Covenant, appropriate to the invoking of blessing from on high, emphasizing and making yet more solemn the prayer which it accompanied. It is thus in principle at one with the use of liturgical rites and ceremonies in general. But the prayer was the essential thing, as St. Augustine saw. Arguing that He who could confer the Holy Ghost must be Himself God, he says: 'For none of His disciples gave the Holy Ghost. They prayed indeed that He might come upon those on whom they laid

---

[1] I Tim. iv. 14.

their hands, they did not give Him themselves. A custom which the Church in the case of its officers retains to this day [1].'

The importance of this point is clear. Let us grant that a certain order is normal, and that it has historical prescription in its favour. Let us grant that at a certain point in history, through an exaggerated reaction largely caused by the fault of those who administered that order, its course was broken and another order substituted. Yet when under that order ministers have been for many generations solemnly set apart and the Divine blessing solemnly invoked upon them by sincere and devout people, not without signs following that the blessing so invoked has been given, even supposing that there was an initial mistake, it seems to me, on a Biblical estimate of the relative value of things, altogether disproportioned to make that initial mistake a cause of fundamental or permanent division.

We shall form a wrong idea if we think of the

---

[1] *De Trin.* xv. 26, § 46 : 'Immo quantus est Deus qui dat Deum ? Neque enim aliquis discipulorum eius dedit Spiritum sanctum. Orabant quippe ut veniret in eos quibus manus imponebant, non ipsi eum dabant. Quem morem in suis praepositis etiam nunc servat Ecclesia.'

growth of the Christian Ministry, with its accompaniments, after the manner of the framing of a written constitution, in which certain leading principles are recognized from the outset and carried out in detail with logical precision. The Christian Ministry, like most other administrative forms, it is probable, rather grew than was made. And that by a process which if we could have seen it we should very likely have described as quite simple and natural—though because natural it is not to be supposed that it is any the less Providential.

There is a good example of this in the next office to which we come, that of the 'elder' or 'presbyter.' It is now, I imagine, generally agreed that this is nothing else than the standing office of the Jewish synagogue transferred to the Christian Church. We are not told anything about the transference, but we find the office existing in the Church at Jerusalem at the time when St. Paul and St. Barnabas arrive with contributions from the Church of Antioch [1].

It could hardly be otherwise. It might conceivably have happened that a whole synagogue, or at least the majority of the congregation,

[1] Acts xi. 30.

came over bodily to Christianity. If so, it would naturally retain its constitution just as it was. But short of this there can be little doubt that some who held the office of presbyter would be converted, and they would certainly not cease to be regarded as presbyters were regarded because they became Christians. The Jewish presbyters apparently were heads of families who took their place as such by right of birth. We read of Paul and Barnabas 'appointing elders' (χειροτονήσαντες πρεσβυτέρους) in the Churches of Lycaonia and Pisidia. But this is what would naturally happen in newly founded Gentile communities modelled at least to that extent upon the Jewish.

Not essentially different would seem to have been the state of things in regard to the remaining order of ἐπίσκοποι or 'bishops.' If we could trace the sequence of events we should probably find that each stage of the history grew out of the last by an unforced and natural process. But unfortunately here there are great gaps in the evidence, and we are left largely to conjecture. We do not know how far the creation of the episcopate in the

---

[1] Acts xiv. 23.

later sense was a deliberate act or under what circumstances it arose. We know that during a period covered by St. Paul's speech at Miletus, the Epistle to the Philippians, the Pastoral Epistles, the Epistle of Clement of Rome, and probably the Shepherd of Hermas, there was a plurality of ἐπίσκοποι in each Church. In other words the terms ἐπίσκοποι and πρεσβύτεροι were applied to the same persons. We know that at the time of the martyrdom of Ignatius, i. e. probably about 110-117 A. D., at Antioch in Syria, and in some of the Churches in Western Asia Minor there was already established a monarchical Episcopate in the later sense. But how the transition was brought about we can only guess.

It is well known how many attempts have been made in recent times to solve this problem. None of them admit of absolute verification. But I confess that to me the most probable theory appears to be that advocated by Dr. Hort, and substantially before him by that most scientific of German scholars, Dr. Loofs, of Halle—the theory, namely, that ἐπίσκοπος was in the first instance not so much the name of an office as a descriptive term, bringing out its characteristic functions[1]. You will see that this at once accounts for the first half of the problem, how it comes about that two words are used to describe the same office.

On this view πρεσβύτερος is the name of the office, and ἐπίσκοπος tells us further that the duty of the presbyter was to exercise over-sight. It is an additional argument in favour of the theory that it is entirely in harmony with the usage of the word up to that date, the end of the first century, both in literature and in inscriptions. ἐπισκοπεῖν, ἐπίσκοπος, ἐπισκοπή are far more common in a general sense than as designating a particular office.

There remains what may be called the second half of the problem—how it was that the plural ἐπίσκοποι, representing a college of presbyters with equal rights, became a single ἐπίσκοπος with superior rights to the rest of the presbytery. This is a still more difficult question than the

---

[1] ' Mir scheint in der vorschnellen Annahme, ἐπίσκοπος sei früher Amtsname, Titel gewesen, ein πρῶτον ψεῦδος vieler neuerer Konstruktionen zu liegen ; die ältere Anschauung halte ich durchaus nicht für veraltet; ἐπίσκοπος ist eine Funktionsbezeich-nung und bis ins endende zweite Jahrhundert hinein gehen die Spuren davon, dass man ein Bewusstsein davon hat dass ἐπίσκοπος weniger Amtsname als Amtsbeschreibung ist' (*Studien u. Kritiken*, 1890, p. 628).

first, and in regard to it we are still more thrown back upon conjecture, as positive data fail us even more completely.

We may think with the older writers of the position of Timothy and Titus as Apostolic delegates, or of St. James as president of the presbyters of Jerusalem, or with Rothe[1] and Löning[2] of Symeon his successor, or with Ramsay[3] of the presbyter whose duty it was to correspond with other Churches (as in the case of Clement of Rome), or with Harnack and Loofs[4] of the presbyter who took the lead in the conduct of worship, especially in the Eucharist. There is no reason for treating these different explanations as alternatives. They all represent causes which were really at work; and they all converge upon the same result. Nor would they exclude the possibility that there were other causes still which have not yet been discovered.

But the important point for us is that if we had been living then we should have seen the episcopate grow up round us—it is very

[1] Cf. Lightfoot, *Philippians*, p. 199 ff.

[2] *Die Gemeindeverfassung des Urchristenthums* (Halle, 1889), p. 116 f.

[3] *Church in the Roman Empire*, p. 367 ff.   [4] Op. cit., p. 652 f.

probable—gradually and imperceptibly from such natural causes as these. It did not drop from the skies. It was not instituted by a voice from heaven. And yet, although it was due —humanly speaking—to the operation of these mediate causes, it may be none the less a Divine ordinance. We no longer think of the Bible as directly dictated to its human authors, and yet we still believe it to be in a most true sense the word of God. And in like manner in regard to the episcopate we may trace its origin to secondary causes, and yet believe that these causes were all the time in the hand of God and carrying out His purposes.

There is, however, another and yet larger question that meets us as soon as we think of the beginnings of formal office in the Christian Church. We are reminded that in the first great age of the Church much that afterwards became the subject of formal office was pro-vided for in another way and by a more direct inspiration. The Epistles of St. Paul, and the Acts read in the light of the Epistles of St. Paul, give us a vivid picture of the forces which really made the Apostolic Age what it was. They are summed up under the general name of the 'Spiritual Gifts.' And to appreciate these gifts at their full value we need further to remember that it was in virtue of their possession of these gifts that St. Paul and St. Peter and St. John, and not only they, but the nameless author of the Epistle to the Hebrews, wrote as they wrote in words that we still read to this day. But it was a peculiarity of these 'Spiritual Gifts' that they were not communicated only through recognized channels. They were so communicated at the prayer of Apostles and others, but that was not the only method of communication. 'The wind bloweth where it listeth, and thou hearest the sound thereof, but canst not tell whence it cometh, and whither it goeth:' even such is the way of the Spirit. Under the Old Covenant there had been sometimes a succession of the prophets, so that one was called and appointed by his predecessor as in the case of Elijah and Elisha. But it was by no means always so. The prophet Amos answered Amaziah, 'I was no prophet, neither was I a prophet's son; but I was an herdman, and a dresser of sycomore trees: and the Lord took me from following the flock, and the Lord said unto me, Go,

prophesy unto My people Israel[1].' The very
greatest prophets, Isaiah, Jeremiah, Ezekiel were
called in this way. And there can be no doubt
that the same double rule held under the
New Covenant as under the Old. There too
Prophecy was a very real thing, and some
prophets received their call and their inspiration
through mediate agencies, and others directly.

The point to be noted is that God has not
only one way of working. He does work
through regular defined channels, but He also
works outside them. And His greatest working
of all has been often of this irregular kind.
This fact, as a fact, we ought to have very
present to our minds.

Yes, I shall be told; but it is a fact—or
a principle rising out of a fact—which it is
extremely dangerous to apply to any century
after the first. At one great extraordinary
conjuncture in the history of the world God
did use extraordinary means to produce extraordinary effects; but the gate is opened
perilously wide if this is taken as a precedent.
We have recently been warned in earnest words
of the risk of allowing a claim to inspiration

[1] Amos vii. 14 f.

simply because it is made[1]. It is well to keep the warning in mind.

Still it cannot cancel the fact that God has in the past been pleased to act in this manner. And I cannot but think that it would be an equal mistake on the other side to limit the range of this action of His strictly to the period embraced within the two covers of the Bible. Outside that period, and outside the bounds of any authorized Ministry there have surely been men, neither prophets nor the sons of prophets, who have been taken as it were from the flocks or the sycomores and have yet done a great work for God and for Christ.

Our Lord Himself laid down a rule which is so simple that the experts in theology have been often tempted to pass it by, though the common sense of the unlearned clings to it. 'Ye shall know them by their fruits.' And applying this test it seems to me that we must speak with very great reserve. It is impossible to condemn those whom God has visibly not condemned.

Let me take one example as typical of all. It is an extreme example in both ways. The Society of Friends meets, I suppose, with the

[1] *Ministerial Priesthood*, p. 110.

most direct negative all those conditions which are most strenuously asserted for a right minis-tration of the Gospel.   They do not acknowledge any visible organization of the Church; they have no regularly constituted Ministry; they dispense with outward Sacraments.   And yet there are few bodies which have upheld such a high and uncompromising standard of Chris-tian practice.   There are few which have lived more consistently up to their beliefs.   There are few which, in proportion to their size, have done more to make Christian principle prevail in the world at large.   I refer of course to their efforts in connexion with slavery, war, and the state of prisons.

Any theory as to the nature of the Christian Ministry must have its place for phenomena—for paradoxes, if we will—like these.   It must not only have a place for them, but it must do justice to them.   But I greatly doubt whether justice can be done by singling out a particular principle and pressing it through in all its logical severity without constant regard to what lies on the right hand and on the left, i.e. to the whole context of its expression in history.

It is a consolation to think that as to the great

fundamental principle of Ministry all Christian men are agreed. Even those of whom I have just spoken as rejecting all outwardly constituted Ministry do so rather from excess than from defect in the assertion of this principle. The principle I mean that the ultimate sanction of all work for God, and the entire enabling of those who desire to work for Him must come from God Himself. This is not in question. And it is I conceive the most essential truth in the claim that is made for the principle of devolution.

Debate begins at the point at which we set about to determine through what precise human channels the Divine sanction and (in a less degree) the Divine enabling should be conveyed. I do not say that this is a matter of indifference. I do not say that here too there is not a more and a less excellent way. All the help and stimulus that can be given us to find that way and to meet upon it when found, is to be greeted with thankfulness. But do not let us by one hand-breadth widen the breach which divides us from our fellow Christians beyond that to which we are absolutely compelled.

NOTE ON CLEM. ROM. *ad Cor.* xliv. 1-3.

IT is contended that although the doctrine of Apostolical Succession is not found in the New Testament, it is laid down so explicitly by St. Clement of Rome as to show that the principle must really date from the time of the Apostles. The passage in question is as follows. I give the Greek text with the ancient Latin version recently discovered by Dom G. Morin.

Καὶ οἱ ἀπόστολοι ἡμῶν ἔγνωσαν διὰ τοῦ Κυρίου ἡμῶν Ἰησοῦ Χριστοῦ ὅτι ἔρις ἔσται ἐπὶ τοῦ ὀνόματος τῆς ἐπισκοπῆς. Διὰ ταύτην οὖν τὴν αἰτίαν πρόγνωσιν εἰληφότες τελείαν κατέστησαν τοὺς προειρημένους, καὶ μεταξὺ ἐπινομὴν ἔδωκαν (or δεδώκασιν) ὅπως, ἐὰν κοιμηθῶσιν, διαδέξωνται ἕτεροι δεδοκιμασμένοι ἄνδρες τὴν λειτουργίαν αὐτῶν. Τοὺς οὖν κατασταθέντας ὑπ' ἐκείνων ἢ μεταξὺ ὑφ' ἑτέρων ἐλλογίμων ἀνδρῶν, συνευδοκησάσης τῆς ἐκκλησίας πάσης, καὶ λειτουργήσαντας ἀμέμπτως

τῷ ποιμνίῳ τοῦ Χριστοῦ . . . τούτους οὐ δικαίως
νομίζομεν ἀποβάλλεσθαι τῆς λειτουργίας.

> ἐπινομήν A Lat. ἐπιδομήν C (cf. Syr.): ἐπιμονήν, adopted
> by Lightfoot, is a conjecture. The accession of
> Lat. to the best MS. seems to establish ἐπινομήν.

'Et apostoli nostri scierunt per Dominum
nostrum Ihesum Christum, quia contentio erit
pro nomine aut episcopatu. Propter hanc
causam prudentiam accipientes perpetuam prae-
posuerunt illos supradictos, et postmodum
legem dederunt, ut si dormierint, suscipiunt
viri alii probati ministerium eorum. Igitur illos
constitutos ab illis vel postmodum a quibusdam
viris ornatis consentiente aecclesia omne (*sic*),
et ministrantes sine querela gregi Christi . . .
hos aestimamus non debere eici ab administra-
tione.'

'And our Apostles knew through our Lord
Jesus Christ that there would be strife over the
name of the bishop's office. For this cause
therefore, having received complete foreknow-
ledge, they appointed the aforesaid persons,
and afterwards gave a further injunction that
if they should fall asleep, other approved men
should succeed to their ministration. Those
therefore who were appointed by them, or
afterwards by other men of repute with the consent of the whole Church, and have ministered
unblamably to the flock of Christ . . . these

men we consider to be unjustly deposed from
their ministration.'

St. Clement is insisting here on the regular
and responsible appointment of the Corinthian
presbyters.   He does not hint in any way at
a transmission of powers.   The ἕτεροι ἐλλόγιμοι
ἄνδρες are not, as some translations of Clement's
language might lead us to suppose, placed on
the direct line of descent from the Apostles.
When we think of the importance of prophecy
and the activity of prophets in the Apostolic
age, it is very improbable that all who held
office or dignity in the Church were appointed to
it directly by Apostles in either the wider or the
narrower sense.   The state of things described
by St. Clement is just what would be natural.
Nominations to office would be made by an
Apostle, if one was available, if not by those
whom the Church most trusted.   But in all
cases the assent of the Church was required.

III

SACERDOTALISM

III

*But I write the more boldly unto you in some measure, as putting
you again in remembrance, because of the grace that was given me of
God, that I should be a minister of Christ Jesus unto the Gentiles,
ministering the gospel of God, that the offering up of the Gentiles
might be made acceptable, being sanctified by the Holy Ghost.*
ROMANS xv. 15, 16.

I SUPPOSE that the deepest cleavage at the
present moment in the Church of England is
that between those who hold and those who
deny the priestly character of the Ministry.
The single word 'Sacerdotalism' indicates the
opposing tendencies. And as it is far more
often on the lips of enemies than on those of
friends, it has contracted an ugly sound that
one would willingly avoid. But it may be best
once and again to adopt the other policy of
looking the difference full in the face, with
a view to see whether it cannot be reduced.
And the belief that it can be greatly reduced

has prompted the words which I am to address to you this morning.

I wish to ask you to consider whether the difference which seems so absolute is not to a greater extent than we are apt to suppose one of names rather than of things; and the inference that I would draw is that if on both sides we steadily resist the temptation to use provocative language, and as steadily compel ourselves to look at the realities that are at issue, instead of the shibboleths which we have come by habit to attach to them, we shall have more of the spirit of brotherhood and of the strength and mutual confidence that comes from it.

I am led to entertain this hope by a book to which I have referred before in this place, and which others besides myself have treated as worthily representing a great cause, Dr. Moberly's *Ministerial Priesthood*. The really central argument in that book is an analysis and discussion of the idea of Priesthood, starting from a criticism of Bishop Lightfoot. Bishop Lightfoot, taking the word 'Priesthood' in a certain sense, had deprecated its use in con- nexion with the Christian Ministry. To this it is replied that the sense thus ascribed to the word is a wrong sense, and another is substituted for it, the applicability of which to the Ministry is strongly affirmed.

I ask you to observe how much of this turns not upon any obstinate conflict of fact or even of ideas, but on the appropriateness of the use of a certain name ; and I ask you to consider how easily the whole argument may be restated without any variation in substance, but with a result which is eirenic instead of controversial. If the sense which Bishop Lightfoot puts upon the word ' Priesthood ' is wrong, it follows that what he deprecates is not what his critic desires to assert, and that what the critic asserts is not what he had deprecated, so that except upon the verbal question they are really argu-ing on different planes, and at bottom it is quite possible that they may be really agreed. I will go further and say that they are to a very large extent agreed, and that a great part of Dr. Moberly's contention is simply common Christian ground, which—apart from the par-ticular way of putting it—may be accepted by men of all parties, and at least raises no party question. It is indeed a significant fact that on the constructive side the writer whom he quotes most freely and with the fullest community of ideas is the late Dr. Milligan, a Presbyterian, though it is true a Presbyterian with exception-ally wide sympathies and exceptional depth of insight.

I do not by what I have said mean to imply that the verbal question is a matter of indiffer-ence or that it is one that may not quite legiti-mately be argued. It is a question that may well touch some tender sensibilities, because on the answer given to it will depend whether language freely used in the Early Church[1] and increasingly used in the Mediaeval Church is justified or abandoned. Besides, it may reason-ably be maintained that a body of ideas is more likely to have justice done to it if it is summed up under a recognized name than if it is only held in a state of tacit and loose acceptance.

I have anticipated thus much in order that the

---

[1] It may be true that sacerdotal language in regard to the Ministry is first employed (so far as we know) by Tertullian in the West and perhaps by Origen in the East, but θυσία (προσφορά) of the Eucharist goes back to the *Didaché* (14 *ter*) and Justin Martyr (*Dial.* 41; cf. 28, 116, 117). The Eucharist was constantly identified by early Christian writers with the θυσία καθαρά of Mal. i. 11 ('in every place incense is offered unto My name, and a pure offering').

drift and tendency of what I am about to say may be clear from the outset. But it is time that we came to close quarters with the controversy as it actually lies before us. Before, however, we can do this with effect there is yet another general question on which it is important to have an understanding.

The discussion of the meaning of words as a first step towards determining truth of ideas is as old as Plato and Aristotle ; but there does not appear to be even yet a satisfactory agreement as to the course which such a discussion should take. It is not sufficiently agreed what is the meaning of a word. Is it what the word is understood to mean in common everyday language ; or is it what the word as a fact means in some typical or classical example ; or is it what the word ought to mean in a comprehensive philosophy of things ?

As between Dr. Moberly and Bishop Lightfoot the ultimate divergence is really of this kind. The question of the Priesthood drives us back upon the further question of the nature of Sacrifice, because the crucial point in the functions of the priesthood is its relation to sacrifice. The burning question as to the Christian

Ministry is precisely this, Is the Christian minister a sacrificing priest, or is he not? If he were merely called 'priest' in the etymological sense of 'presbyter,' there would be no controversy. It is when the claim is made that the functions of the priest include sacrifice that controversy begins.

Now, in seeking to determine this point, it cannot be considered unnatural that Bishop Lightfoot should go to the Old Testament institution of sacrifice. The Old Testament presents us with a typical example of a priesthood, the leading function of which is the offering of sacrifice. This supplies the standard to which Bishop Lightfoot refers when he denies that function to the Christian priesthood. I submit that in so doing he is at least not open to censure. A process so exceedingly natural, so broadly intelligible, so directly in touch with the instincts of the plain man cannot be otherwise than legitimate. And his conclusion, limited as it obviously must be, is nothing less than self-evident: the Christian Ministry is not a sacrificing priesthood in the Old Testament sense of sacrifice.

But it is also a legitimate inquiry to ask

whether behind the Old Testament institution of sacrifice, behind the Pagan sacrifices, behind sacrifice as an institution in all its forms, there is not an idea of sacrifice purified from all grosser elements, independent of all the blood of beasts shed on Jewish or Pagan altars, a pattern of sacrifice laid up in the heavens and invested with none but heavenly attributes, which may be fulfilled as much and indeed far more in Christianity than in Judaism. This is what Dr. Moberly contends for. He starts from the fact that the Death of Christ is described as a sacrifice;—and it is one of his points that the conception of sacrifice in the case of Christ is not to be too closely identified with His death ; the death is an element in it, a necessary and unavoidable element under the given conditions, but not the whole or even the greatest part of it. The offering of Himself to the Father by our Lord Jesus Christ was an act of sacrifice. It had so much in common with the Mosaic sacrifices that without death it would have been incomplete and ineffectual for its purpose : 'Without shedding of blood there is no re-mission.' Christ therefore died, and through death made good His sacrifice. But what Christ does, that the Church, which is the body of Christ, also does. And what the Church does, that the Ministry, who are its executive organs, also do. It follows that the New Covenant has its sacrificial system as well as the Old. And that system is not only concentrated upon the single act of Christ but permeates the whole society, and within the society finds its special expression in the Priesthood.

Let us pause for a moment over these last two steps where the reasoning may well seem to be somewhat removed from ordinary apprehension. There is a certain cycle of teaching the essence of which is really common to St. Paul and St. John, though the language in which it is expressed is different, and hints of it are given under the yet simpler forms of the Synoptic Gospels. The imitation of Christ is no merely external thing. It is, or it should be, an inner appropriation, assimilation, and reproduction of the law of the life of Christ. That law is in its root and essence *dying in order to live*. The Christian does not die in order to live exactly in the full and transcendent sense in which Christ died. His Death and His Rising again were charged with a world-wide significance. They had relation to the whole human race. In that they were unique. The Christian follows in his Master's steps afar off. But he too, so far as in him lies, must '*die with Christ*' as St. Paul expresses it. He must die to sin; he must put off 'the old man'; he must struggle to free himself from the meshes of temptation through the flesh in which he is involved. He must do all this not in his own strength but in the strength of Christ, on whom his affections are so concentrated that it is as if Christ and he were actually one.

This is what St. John means, or what our Lord Himself means in the version of St. John, when He says 'I am the way'—a text so impressively expounded in the *Hulsean Lectures* of Dr. Hort. It is really what the Synoptists also mean when they speak of losing the life in order to find it—that is losing the lower life, the life dominated by the senses, in order to gain the higher life, the life dominated by the Spirit.

All this, as I have said, is common Christian doctrine—doctrine it is true, which belongs to a high region of thought and of endeavour to which it is hard for the average man to attain, but yet which may be attained in indefinitely

various degrees, and which is often attained more
fully in practice than it could be consciously
explained in theory. At least it corresponds to
no divisions of party.

Neither is there any party division really
involved, though we may seem to be coming
nearer to it, when we pass on with Dr. Moberly
to speak of the ceremonial appropriation of the
Death of Christ. If the Christian is to be made
one with Christ in His Death, there can be no
doubt that the ceremonial expression of this is
to be sought in the Holy Communion. Whatever we may think as to the exact method by
which the sacrament operates, we must all,
whether Churchmen or Nonconformists, regard
it as the one appointed ceremonial means, the
only ceremonial means under the New Covenant,
of realizing to ourselves the Death of Christ.
This is undoubtedly what St. Paul intends when
he says, 'The cup of blessing which we bless,
is it not a communion of the blood of Christ?
The bread which we break, is it not a communion
of the body of Christ[1]?'

We may rate higher or we may rate lower
the value of ceremonial means, but in any case

[1] 1 Cor. x. 16.

thus much is clear. The sacrament of the Lord's Supper is common to nearly all Christians, and whatever else it may denote, it denotes certainly this, the bringing home of the Death and Sacrifice of Christ to the soul of man.

I do not see that any reasonable exception can be taken to the view that the Church in its acts of Eucharistic worship identifies itself with the Death of Christ; and it is but a natural step from this to say that it does this through an ordained ministry as its organs.

The language that one commonly hears from those who would be thought to hold high doctrine on these subjects is somewhat different, though in effect it is the same. It is usually said that the minister in the sacrament 'pleads' or 'presents' the Sacrifice of Christ; and it is by virtue of this pleading or presenting of a sacrifice that he is himself described as 'sacrificing.'

I submit, however, that to sacrifice and to 'plead' or 'present' a sacrifice ceremonially are really distinct things. And if those who think with Bishop Lightfoot took their stand upon this distinction, and said that in a strict use of terms those who do but plead or present the Sacrifice of Another are not entitled to speak or be spoken of as though the act of sacrifice were their own, their position would seem to be inexpugnable.

All turns ultimately upon the relation of the one great and true Sacrifice and the shadows of it that are enacted upon earth, but enacted by the express institution of Him by whom the Sacrifice was made. It seems to me that the clergy of the Church of England are really loyal in this matter. I do not believe that even the very 'highest' among them would wish to infringe upon the uniqueness of the great Sacrifice. There is not one who would say that that Sacrifice needed to be *repeated*. How could it possibly need to be repeated? It is an eternal act, done once for all, but with an effect that is indestructible. Dr. Moberly well says, speaking of the sense in which the Son is said to plead His own Sacrifice to the Father, ' The words "pleading" or "presenting" in this connexion must not be understood as describing anything corresponding to specific acts done, or words spoken by Christ in His glory. His glorified presence *is* an eternal presentation; He pleads by what He *is*[1].'

The Church of Rome has gone furthest in a questionable direction when it declares the Eucharist to be *verum ac proprium sacrificium* and *vere propitiatorium*; and there can be no doubt .that it has given cause for a great amount of popular misunderstanding of a very serious kind. But I am not sure that even the language of the Church of Rome is not capable so far of being reconciled with truth. Even the Church of Rome would allow that in the last resort that which it calls a 'sacrifice' is such as being identified with the Sacrifice of Christ [2]. Its virtue is derivative and not original.

I understand that in Dr. Moberly's conception the element of 'sacrifice' in the work of the Ministry would be twofold. On the one hand there is the ceremonial or sacramental act of sacrifice which is wholly of this derived character, and has for its background the true Sacrifice of Christ. And on the other hand there is the appropriation of the spirit of Christ's Sacrifice—that which gave it its value, the spirit of self-devotion and love. The minis-

---

[1] *Ministerial Priesthood*, p. 246 n.   [2] Ibid., p. 231.

terial life ought, it is urged, to be a constant
expression of this spirit taking the form of
pastoral care. The Christian minister should
be no mere performer of an *opus operatum*; he
should live for his people, and let himself spend
and be spent in their service.

Are we called upon in any way to dispute
this conception? The only question which it
seems to me can rightly be raised in regard
to it is whether it sufficiently corresponds to
what is commonly understood by sacrifice,
and whether it has sufficient warrant in the
language of the New Testament. I confess to
some reluctance to reading back the ideas of
succeeding centuries into the New Testament.
History is full of grooves which we must get
out of if we would secure any real freshness
of apprehension. Continuity is a good thing,
and we may see the hand of God in history;
and yet we cannot forget that an element of
human perversity and fallibility enters in. The
development which began in the second century
ends in the state of things before the Reformation. It is a delicate and laborious matter
to separate the strands of good and evil, of
truth and error. We may then be glad, where

we can, to escape the necessity for doing this by going back beyond the point at which they begin to be closely intertwined. The appeal to Scripture is a common ground where we can meet some who will not be so ready to meet us when the Scriptures are left behind.

We ask then if the conception of the Christian Ministry of which we have been speaking has, or has not, a Scriptural sanction. Does the New Testament sufficiently recognize it in the character of a priesthood, and of a sacrificing priesthood ? I think we may say that it does. I doubt if there is any passage so strong as the verse which I have chosen for my text. The sacrificial terminology is far more marked in the original than it can be in a translation. St. Paul is apologizing to the Roman Christians for his boldness in urging upon them their duties. It is not as if he were preaching some new thing ; he is only recalling to their minds what they already know. And he does this in virtue of the Apostleship of the Gentiles which has been committed to him. ' I write,' he says, ' because of the grace that was given me of God, that I should be a minister of Christ Jesus unto the Gentiles' ($\lambda\epsilon\iota\tau\text{o}\upsilon\rho\gamma\grave{o}\nu$ $X\rho\iota\sigma\tau\text{o}\hat{\upsilon}$ '$I\eta\sigma\text{o}\hat{\upsilon}$ $\epsilon\emph{i}s$

τὰ ἔθνη—I need not remind you that λειτουργόν is exactly the word that would be used of the discharge of the priests' office in the Temple), 'ministering the gospel of God' (the R. V. notes in the margin that the Greek is 'ministering in sacrifice'—the word is ἱερουργοῦντα, the technical term for the function of sacrifice), 'that the offering up of the Gentiles' (ἡ προσφορὰ τῶν ἐθνῶν, i. e. not 'the offering which the Gentiles *make*, but which the Gentiles *are*') 'might be made acceptable, being sanctified by the Holy Ghost.' The Apostle conceives of himself as standing at the altar; and the offering which he lays upon the altar is the Gentile Church, so far as it is of his founding or comes within his special province.   An offering ought to be without blemish.   It ought to be first purified before it is offered.   And it is the Apostle's earnest prayer to God, that these converts of his, these Gentile Churches for which he is responsible, may be so sanctified by the outpouring of the Holy Spirit upon them that they may be an offering really acceptable, a sacrifice of a sweet smelling savour, for the purpose for which they are destined.

Is not this really very much the conception

of Priesthood expounded by Dr. Moberly?
There is the same double aspect, the ceremonial
and the moral. For if it is said that the language
of St. Paul is metaphor, a figure of speech and
not of act, that is but a superficial distinction.
All ceremonial is based on symbolism, and the
symbolism of act is only more effective than
the symbolism of word. But in this particular
case the symbolism of word is so clear and vivid,
that action itself could hardly make it more
forcible. We seem to see the battered and
shattered Apostle, in bodily presence weak, but
uplifted by the strength of deeply felt emotion,
pouring out his whole soul to God as he lays
this offering of his upon the altar, wrestling in
prayer for the precious souls which he has won
from destruction and commending them to the
most effectual working of Divine grace, that
they may fulfil the true end of their being, the
glory of God who made and redeemed them.

There we see how the ceremonial act is really
expressive of the moral. It is the fervour of
the soul finding outward utterance. In Dr. Moberly's definition of sacrifice it is this fervour,
this devotion of the soul which is the essential
thing. That is why he lays such very great

stress on the pastoral side of the Priesthood. A priesthood without the pastoral side, is to him no priesthood at all. Unless in some way or other it finds an equivalent, it is a ministry professedly sacrificial but wanting just that element of sacrifice which gives it reality, which gives it the true worth of sacrifice in the sight of God.

If the Sacrifice of the Son of God is really His Love going forth and treading the winepress alone in a world of sorrow and sin, then the sacrificing Priesthood, if the Christian Ministry deserve the august name, is such by virtue of the distant gleams which it reflects of the Divine Sacrifice. It has no original virtue; it has no mechanical virtue; it must enter, however imperfectly, into the sphere of the great Divine purpose of which it forms part, if it is to discharge its functions at all.

When the doctrine of a 'sacrificing Priesthood' is presented in this way, I confess that I do not see why any of us should quarrel with it. I do not think that we do quarrel with it. If that sainted bishop—a true saint for simplicity and singleness of aim, though he spent his days in no cloister but in the active work of scholarship and administration—if he, who brought out the stores of his learning to combat what is commonly known as ' sacerdotalism,' could arise and be questioned and have this theory of ' Ministerial Priesthood ' set before him, I fully believe that he would not condemn but welcome it. What he combated, and what the strenuous opponents of sacerdotalism still combat, is, I believe, a wholly different thing. It is that spirit of clerical arrogance and assumption [1], utterly alien to the real leaders of the movement and to all who really understand their own meaning, of which the doctrines called ' sacerdotal ' are the excuse and not the cause. It is difficult to see how a book like *Ministerial Priesthood*, so carefully guarded, so critical and severe in its ideal of ministerial duty, could furnish even a pretext for such perversion.

I fail to see myself how the question is even one of a greater or less degree of ritual. Tastes differ largely as to the extent to which they would choose to have ideas presented to the eye and to the ear as well as to the mind. But if the ideas that underlie the presentation are

---

[1] The legal doctrine that a benefice is the freehold of the incumbent for the time being is sometimes applied in a way that is very repellent. But this is neither Churchmanship nor Christianity.

not harmful, the mode of presentation does not make them harmful. At least we should exercise a large-minded charity in judging upon such matters, and make full allowance for difference of temperament and mental constitution.

There is, I quite believe, a danger—a real danger—of materialized views of spiritual things, especially of the Sacrament. But the book of which I have been speaking is full of protests against such views. Nor would it be difficult to find abundant protests coming from the same side. If I may say so, I regard these protests as of especial value, because they come from quarters from which advice and remonstrance will be listened to. It is better for those of us who can speak with less of sympathy to keep silent.

For it is, after all, not so easy as it may seem to say where materialism begins. The exact limits and relations of material and spiritual form a philosophical problem of which perhaps even the thinkers have not got to the bottom, much less those who are not thinkers. It may well be that those who seem to err on the side of materialism are at the bottom of their minds seeking to assert and emphasize their sense of the reality of sacramental grace, of which they have personal experience and conviction. If they do not deceive themselves, if they do not let the outward take the place of the inward, if they show the true fruits of the Spirit, we may give them credit for sincerity, and receive what they may say with the respect to which all genuine conviction is entitled.

A more tender place is touched by the exclu-sive claims which are made for the apostolically descended priesthood. It is the negative side of these claims which is felt, the denial of the right of those who have not the same descent. This really cuts to the quick, and we cannot for a moment wonder that it should do so.

But even here there is room to hope that some steps are possible towards an under-standing. In the first place, it should be distinctly borne in mind that the more sweeping refusal to recognize the non-episcopal Reformed Churches is not, and can never be made, a doctrine of the Church of England. Too many of her most representative men have not shared in it. Hooker did not hold it; Andrewes ex-pressly disclaimed it[1]; Cosin freely communicated

---

[1] The views of these writers appear to me, so far as I can judge, to be fairly and correctly presented in Dr. Brown's *Apostolical Succession*, p. 404 ff.

with the French Reformed Church during his exile. Indeed, it is not until the last half of the present century that more than a relatively small minority of English Churchmen have been committed to it.

Again, those who within this period have taken up the negative position have done so in no lightness of heart, but in deference to what they conceive to be an absolutely constraining logic, and they have done it with the amplest possible acknowledgement of Christian excellences in the separated bodies.

Further, it will be noted that the more responsible writers avoid as far as possible the use of language which involves any sort of judgement upon these bodies. For instance, when Dr. Moberly asserts that a certain form of Church organization is 'essential' or 'indispensable,' he is careful to add that he means 'essential, or indispensable *for us*'—for those brought up as we are, who can accept the premisses from which he is arguing. He always has in view the reservation that God is not bound by His own appointed methods—that 'outside His appointed "media" of whatever kind—ministries, sacraments, ordinances—

He can work, if He will, as divinely as within them.' This consideration, he adds, may serve 'somewhat to the lowliness of our thoughts; it may abash us from the presumption of even imagining, at any time, anything like a judgement of others, whose case before God is known to Him, not to us[1].' I have said that the responsible writers and speakers do not often forget this. It were only to be wished that the same caution would extend more completely to the rank and file. It would save them not only from exciting much just resentment against the Church of which they boast, but also from many a departure from Christian humility and charity in themselves.

Lastly, it seems to follow that if at any time those who hold these views are compelled to express them, a more guarded and appropriate way of speaking would be, not to 'unchurch' the bodies that do not satisfy all their requirements, but to speak of them rather as 'Churches with a certain defect of order or organization.' Where there are so many signs of God's presence the impugned bodies must needs have a right to be called 'Churches.' And

[1] *Ministerial Priesthood*, p. 61.

H

the saving clause would leave the nature and gravity of the defect to the judgement of God.

If the members of these bodies could see that with those who hold such opinions they are not taken up wantonly or in a spirit of mere hostility, that they are no product of pride or presumption, but a severe and unwelcome necessity of thought, their natural anger would by degrees give way to sorrowful acquiescence.

For I also cannot but think that at least our own Nonconformists will by degrees come round to feel that there is something unsatisfactory in their own position. I may claim that they are for the most part at one with us in the principle that there should be some differentiation of function between ministers and people. Most of them recognize that the minister cannot rightly assume office to himself, that he needs to be called by the Church and solemnly admitted with prayer for God's blessing. Most Nonconformist bodies would go as far as this ; and then, as the growing study of history among them extends and deepens, they will I believe further come to see that the Episcopal organization was the rule of the Church for fifteen centuries, that in practice it has many recommendations, and that the reasons for which in the sixteenth century it was thrown over were insufficient. They might come in the end to reach hands to those of us who hold that although Episcopacy is not of divine right it is yet the normal order, a sound link in the chain which binds us to the Great Church of the past.

However that may be, I feel sure that as time goes on, we shall all, Anglican and Nonconformist alike, find ourselves compelled to confess that in some respects the reaction of the sixteenth century went further than it need have gone. The excuses were great; they could hardly have been greater. The uprising of the Northern nations was an uprising in the name of pure religion, and pure religion has upon the whole been the gainer. But we must say 'on the whole'; and the balance is perhaps not so clear and decisive as in our self-complacency we are apt to assume. There was an element of exaggeration and fanaticism in the Reformation, and there was a not inconsiderable uprooting of wheat with the tares.

The verdict is not mine; it is not that of any individual, however learned and however authoritative. It is the verdict of that impersonal force, the voice of which is becoming clearer and more certain every day, the verdict of really impartial History. The figure of History sits enthroned in the clouds; the weapons of our partisanship cannot touch her, and our efforts to escape from her are vain; her word once deliberately issued is inexorable.

Before the bar of History all our conflicting sects and parties will have in the end to lay their several pleas, and await the verdict in silence. I do not doubt that we shall all have many sins and shortcomings to confess. We shall have to abase ourselves in dust and ashes. But the same Power before whom we do this, if it cannot give us absolution will at least give us consolations. I have spoken of the confession which, if I am not greatly mistaken, the Anglican in his degree and the Nonconformist also in his degree, will have one day to make. But we are not alone: the proudest and greatest of all the Churches is at our side.

Listen to a few sentences from the closing paragraphs of a History of the Christian Church by a Roman Catholic professor, who is one of that band, gathered from many nations and many tongues, by whom the impersonal voice is gradually taking articulate shape :—

'The development of events must fill us with sadness. The Christian heart yearns not for separation but for unity. . . . Especially deplorable for us Westerns is the disruption of the sixteenth century. And yet, much as it may trouble us, it was not without salutary consequences. The question has often been asked whether the reform of the Church would ever have been brought about without it. We cannot answer absolutely in the negative, for that would be to doubt the vitality of the Church and its providential guiding. But just as little can it be disputed that the reform had been waited for much too long, and that it did not come until the edifice of the Church had been shaken to its very foundations and until there had been a great falling away. History shows further that the reform was not only carried into execution after this falling away, but that it was also brought on and hastened in its course by it. The revival of the Church is thus presented as closely associated with the disruption. . . . Even the confusion of creeds (*Mischung der Konfessionen*) which has succeeded to the older un-challenged unity (*Abgeschlossenheit*) in the recent period, has not proved to be a mere evil though it has brought with it many abuses. In the countries invaded by it, the religious life at least pulsates at the present time more vigorously than in the rest. The fact is indisputable, and its explanation lies near at hand. The opposition of the confessions incites to greater care and to stronger efforts.'

Can we expect a more magnanimous ad-mission? Does it not touch the very heart of the matter? And does it not justify the belief that the truth of history heals wounds if it makes them? For the rest I do not think that we can do better than adopt, both in their patience and in their faith, the concluding words of all: 'These consequences put a more favourable appearance on that development than it at first sight presents. Nevertheless the disruption must be regarded as an evil; indeed it is on all sides felt as such, and that, not only by Catholics, but by many thousands of Protestants. But there it is, and there, as far as we can see, it is likely for a long time yet to remain. Under these circumstances we must meanwhile seek comfort in these consequences, but above all trust firmly in the Lord of the Church, who although His dealings with us children of men are dark, yet always keeps His hand protectingly over that which He has founded, true to the word which He spake to His disciples, " I am with you alway, even unto the end of the world[1]."

[1] Funk, *Lehrbuch der Kirchengeschichte* (3rd ed., 1898), p. 589 f.

IV

THE PRESENT SITUATION

IV

Now I beseech you, brethren, through the name of our Lord Jesus Christ, that ye all speak the same thing, and that there be no divisions among you; but that ye be perfected together in the same mind and in the same judgement. I COR. i. 10.

ONE of the most remarkable things about St. Paul is his extreme sensitiveness to all the influences for good or for evil at work upon the Church[1]. His mind is like one of those delicate instruments invented by modern science which registers the slightest change in the atmosphere around it, and feels as if from afar the approach of disturbance or trouble. Whole volumes are contained in those touching words with which he closes the catalogue of his bodily sufferings in the cause of Christ. These alone are such as even the most energetic and the most daring of later missionaries could

[1] The situation contemplated in this sermon is that of August 14, when the sermon was preached.

hardly parallel; but they are after all only one
department of the Apostle's experience. 'Beside
those things that are without,' he writes, 'there
is that which presseth upon me daily, anxiety
for all the churches. Who is weak, and I am
not weak? who is made to stumble, and
I burn not[1]?' The Epistles that have come
down to us are an eloquent comment upon this
passage. We may see in them how St. Paul
seems to have had spread out before him a
mental map—or shall we say photograph—of
the Church to which he is writing. He knows
each individual member of it by name, and not
only knows him by name but he knows what
is passing in his mind. He can see all the
currents of thought or feeling which agitate
the little society—for we must remember that
although the Churches of St. Paul's own foundation were very numerous, each one of them as
judged by our present standards would have
seemed very small. Not only the greater
storms, the more violent divisions which none
could fail to see, but even the lightest breath
which ruffled the surface of these St. Paul saw.
It filled him with anxiety. He must needs

[1] 2 Cor. xi. 28 f.

himself personally intervene; and he would not rest until the danger had subsided.

Here at the beginning of the First Epistle to the Corinthians we have an instance of one of the greater convulsions—the Church split up as it were, into four hostile factions—one saying 'I am of Paul,' and one 'I am of Apollos,' and a third 'I of Cephas,' and a fourth 'I of Christ.' So far has the rupture gone that the Apostle exclaims indignantly, 'Is Christ divided? was Paul crucified for you? or were ye baptized into the name of Paul[1]?' In the Second Epistle to the same Church, we have a more subtle and complicated state of things— a state of things so subtle and complicated that for us, and from the hints which the Apostle gives, it is difficult to unravel; but we can see that just because there was no single openly declared issue but secret influences were undermining the Church, and that on a wide scale, his anxiety was increased, and was at the moment very acute indeed.

We pass over from Corinth to a Church like Philippi, the general condition of which was very satisfactory, but even there private feuds

[1] I Cor. i. 13.

appear to have run high. 'I exhort Euodia, and I exhort Syntyche, to be of the same mind in the Lord[1].' The Apostle pours out the whole affectionateness of his nature in earnest entreaty, 'If there is therefore any comfort in Christ, if any consolation of love, if any fellowship of the Spirit, if any tender mercies and compassions, fulfil ye my joy, that ye be of the same mind, having the same love, being of one accord, of one mind[2].' These concluding words in their iteration of the same idea remind us strongly of the verse which I took for my text. They show how very much St. Paul had at heart the unity of the Church—its unity in every sense, both large and small—as well in the relation of individuals to each other as of party to party. St. Paul would have been the last to deprecate variety. He understood too well how the body is composed of many members, and each member has a different function. But he is very urgent that these various members should work together smoothly and harmoniously. That is the true type of the working of a living body, a body that is not only alive but healthy and vigorous in its life.

[1] Phil. iv. 2.   [2] Phil. ii. 1 f.

Measured by this Apostolic standard, what shall we say as to the course of things in our own National Church within the last twenty-five years and at the present time? I take twenty-five years because it was, roughly speaking, at about that distance of time that our Church might have seemed to a bystander to be most divided against itself[1]. A number of bitter controversies were then on foot which had not been decided. High was against Low, and Low against High, and both against Broad. Strenuous endeavours were made by each party to suppress one or other of its neighbours.

Happily, as I cannot but think, those efforts did not succeed. And if we were to try to characterize the last quarter of a century in the Church of England, I suppose we might say that its chief characteristic has been a steady approximation and reconciliation of party to party. Each has come to recognize more and more the virtues of the others; and each has tried more and more to assimilate those virtues for itself. We often hear it remarked to what an extent good Evangelical doctrine is preached from High

---

[1] The Public Worship Regulation Act was passed in 1874.

Church pulpits. The reason is because there is real support for that doctrine in Holy Scripture; and honest clear-sighted men could not but see that there was this support, and could not but act upon what they saw. In quite an equal degree the mass of the Evangelical party has altered its tone towards High Churchmen, because they saw that they too really did love the Lord Jesus in sincerity, and because they saw the fruit of their labours visibly impressed upon many a slum and alley throughout the land. Much too was due to a more open-minded reading of history and a stronger sense of the value to a Church of historic continuity. The Broad Church party hardly exists any longer in the way in which it did when its leading members were fighting for bare life against attacks from this side and from that. But why has it so far ceased to exist? Because it has been crushed and exterminated? No; but because the greater part of its work is done. It has leavened the thought of its opponents, and the causes that it advocated are now taken up under other flags than its own. All this has been progress of the best kind—what was admirably described from this pulpit a few Sundays ago[1] as—'not compromise for the sake of peace but comprehension for the sake of truth.'

But now, just at the present moment, there appears to be a check in the process of approximation and assimilation. I do not think that the check as a whole is serious; but there are perhaps one or two features in it which are serious, and in any case it is well to look the situation in the face.

I do not know whether I interpret rightly the tenor of opinion among the great body of those not immediately concerned, but the interpretation which I should put upon it would be something like this.

Few would approve of the scenes which have taken place or of the particular kind of protest against certain practices which has been adopted. At the same time, it has been regarded with more tolerance than would have been extended to it if it had not been felt that the protesters were sincere, if narrow, and not very well advised or scrupulous men. It has also been felt that they had, from their point of view, a real grievance, and that they

[1] By the Rev. C. G. Lang, Vicar of Portsea, at the time of the Lectures to Clergy.

had some excuse in the difficulty of attracting public attention, which unfortunately is too often done most effectually by creating a scandal.

On the other hand, the things protested against have not been so severely condemned as they might have been, partly because the individuals concerned had credit for being in other respects good and hard-working men, and partly because it is coming to be understood that every great movement is sure to have a fringe of extravagance round it, which must be set down to the general frailty of human nature, and must not necessarily condemn the movement with which it is associated.

Then again, the events in question have called forth spontaneous expressions of loyalty from representatives of the main body of the party implicated, which have had a reassuring effect. At bottom, the nation as a whole knows what it really owes to that party, and its natural temper is one of tolerance where it thinks that much good is purchased by a little harm.

I do not think that the disturbances of which we have heard so much have been more than a nine days' wonder, such as soon subsides again into quiet. And I doubt if even the cry of lawlessness in the Church with which they have been connected, will have had any further effect than a little wholesome tightening of the reins and a strengthening of the hands of lawful authority. This is indeed a thing to be desired. Freedom is a good thing, but one of our dangers at the present day is lest freedom should degenerate into licence.

In all this I do not see any substantial bar to that steady advance which is making our Church more compact, more united, a stronger and a better instrument for doing the work of God in the world. I attach more significance to an influence of another kind.

Of course we know that there are two extreme sections in the Church diametrically opposed to each other. At present, one of these is active in attack, and the other is on its defence. We cannot be surprised if the attacking party, seeing the present conjuncture to be more favourable for it than circumstances have been for some time past, should put forth all its strength and use all its weapons. One of the most effective of these weapons is, I suspect, the publication of a book entitled *The Secret History of the Oxford Movement*[1].

We cannot help being reminded of another *History of the Oxford Movement* by the late Dean of St. Paul's. Only one word is added to the title, but the tendency of the two books is almost directly opposed. I do not doubt that in the process of approximation and assimilation, of which I have spoken, Dean Church's book has played a prominent part. Every one felt that, whatever the ultimate value of the movement which it described, it was at least the meeting-point of a great amount of high-minded aspiration and endeavour. There was an elevation, a chastened and high-toned dignity about the picture, which exercised a great power of attraction over those whose sympathies had not hitherto been enlisted. It was a book the effect of which was healing, reconciling, uniting. It drew Churchmen together, because it set before them an ideal which all felt that they would be proud and glad to make their own.

[1] By Walter Walsh, London, 1897.

The effect of *The Secret History of the Oxford Movement* would be on the contrary—at least if it were read without discrimination—rather to disunite than to unite, to discredit one large section of the Church, to undermine and destroy its influence.

The author himself would not, I think, disclaim this object in writing. And his book has been taken up and is, I believe, being circulated widely by those who openly profess to have that object. Now, a book will no doubt work far more quietly than sensational scenes in church or before a magistrate, but I do not on that account consider it the less but rather the more really formidable. And this particular book seems to me very much calculated to have the effect which is sought. For I must do the author the justice to say that he has written calmly and temperately. He has expressed a great desire to be fair towards those whom he criticizes and not to misrepresent them. There may be different opinions as to what constitutes fairness; but so far as it consists in an appeal to documents, the claim in this instance cannot be denied.

Nor am I sure that the publication of a work like this is wholly to be regretted. If it had come much earlier—twenty or thirty or forty years ago—it might have shaken the edifice of our Church more seriously than it can do now. And in itself perhaps it is well that some things should be known which have hitherto been more or less concealed. I do not blame too much either the conceal-ment or the publication. All depends upon the temper in which the whole indictment is received by us, the general public or main body of the Church, who stand apart from either side.

For we must take the book as an indictment—and an indictment with evidence alleged. This is the first caution which I think that we ought to bear in mind. The whole statement is *ex parte*, a deliberate collection of facts the object of which is to discredit opponents. If I do not call it exactly unfair, it is because there is a proverb that 'all things are fair in war,' and here the two sides are practically at war. The one is seeking of set purpose to injure and depress the other.

Facts that are really facts may be so stated as

to do serious injustice. In the present case all the stress is laid on the supposed 'secrecy' of the movement, and everything that can be called in any sense 'secret' is marshalled in evidence against it. But how many things may be described as 'secret' which are yet perfectly free from blame on account of their secrecy!

Let us consider. In the first place, it is not only natural, but right, that what aims at the deepening of the inner religious life should be conducted quietly, and not obtruded before the eye of the world. The instinct of reverence impels a devout mind to keep such things to itself, especially when that which it regards as sacred would not be equally so regarded by others. Our Lord Himself bade His disciples exercise great care and discretion in exposing the mysteries of their religion to heathen and unbelievers. He compared this to giving holy things to dogs or casting pearls before swine [1]. And although it would be harsh and wrong to apply this saying directly to those whose worst defect may be a certain narrowness and callousness, due as much to training as to nature, still the principle holds good. The refinements of

[1] Matt. vii. 6.

worship exist only for those who can enter into their spirit. It would be in vain to offer them where they would be received without intelligence and without sympathy.

Another form which the charge of secrecy takes has reference to the appearance of duplicity in those who have become converts to the Church of Rome. It is said that up to the last moment they have used language which must have been insincere, both of the communion which they were leaving and of that which they were about to join. But who shall be the judge in such cases? Hardly those who have never undergone a mental crisis of the kind. Such are apt to forget that there must needs be a double strain in the thought of those who have made so momentous a change, both sides of which are perfectly sincere. They are indeed all the time arguing with themselves. There are two voices within; and if the exigencies—or, if we will, temptations—of the position lead one to speak aloud while the other is only heard in the silent court of conscience, that is not exactly insincerity. The most eminent of all the converts to Rome in this century laid bare his soul in this matter, and the verdict of his countrymen has acquitted him of serious blame, where it did not so wholly acquit one of his colleagues.

Lastly, it is sought to base a damaging charge on the production of books which, by the very nature of their object, had a limited and guarded circulation. It is not difficult to place such things in an invidious light. But it does not follow that everything which is innocent in itself will bear to be proclaimed from the housetop, or that all that cannot be so proclaimed must therefore in itself be mischievous. There may be some danger, but it has certainly been much exaggerated.

I pass on to another, and a still more important caution. The author of the book of which I am speaking has mixed up together a number of practices which stand upon a very different footing, and he embraces in one sweeping condemnation many societies and classes of persons in regard to which others of us would feel the necessity for careful discrimination.

The reason in his case is deep-seated. He regards everything that has any resemblance to the practice of the Church of Rome as wrong: he does not ask if it is bad, or pre-

ponderantly bad, in itself. It is enough for him
that it has the stamp of Rome.

No doubt in taking up this position he is
doing what very many Englishmen have done
for a long time past. He appeals to a prejudice
in which he will find plenty of sympathizers.
But this position is distinctly not that of the
English Church ; and it is a position which many
others, out of no partiality for Rome but in
the interests of sheer justice and truth, have
felt compelled to abandon.

I say, first, that the position in question is
not that of the Church of England. Even in
the days before our Church had reached a clear
self-consciousness of the principles of its own
being, when it was still feeling its way towards
the ground which Hooker and Overall and
Andrewes gradually defined for it, it did not
appeal to the Scriptures alone but to the
Scriptures and Antiquity. No other Reformed
Church kept in view the usage of the early
centuries so steadily and so persistently [1]. The

[1] It would be an interesting inquiry, which it may be hoped
that some student of this period may some day undertake, to
compare the history of the appeal to Antiquity in the Lutheran
and Anglican communions. No doubt both began by making the
appeal, but the divergence would seem to have been early felt—

statements made as to ancient practice will not always hold water, but it was agreed that that practice—the practice of the Church of the first four general Councils—when it could be ascertained, was binding. But this principle covered a number of things which the more advanced Reformers objected to as Roman. In fact it might be said that the Church of England only discarded what express proof of Holy Scripture compelled it to discard; whereas of Calvin and Zwingli it would be true to say that they only retained what express proof of Holy Scripture compelled them to retain[1].

at least if we may trust Barlowe's *Dialogue on the Lutheran Factions* (ed. Lunn, p. 71): 'In denyenge purgatorye and auctorite of yᵉ pope, yf they founde in auncyent auctours as much as a corrupte tytle of a pystle sownynge any thynge to theyr purpose, all be it the Epystle selfe made whole against it: yet wold they take it as the worde of god and sure reuelation of the spyryte. Contrarye wyse, yf anye alledged Austen, Hierome, Cypryane, or Chrysostome agaynste them they wolde admytte theyr sentences for none auctoryte, sayenge they were men, and all men were lyers.' Barlowe's *Dialogue* was published after a visit to Germany in 1531, and reprinted (without alteration) in 1553. It seems, however, that Barlowe not only mixed with Lutherans proper but that he also went into 'hye Almayne unto the Oecolampadians, and remaynynge there amonge them was oftentymes conuersaunt with yᵉ Anabaptistes'; so that we cannot be sure that he does not mix up different opinions.

[1] There is a significant passage in a letter of Cranmer's, written —it will be noted—in 1552, when he had gone as far as he ever

You will observe the broad difference between these two positions. The one sacrificed many an innocent and primitive usage which the other preserved, or marked as worthy of preservation.

It is true, however, that in the early years of Queen Elizabeth there were many earnest people, especially among those who had been exiles for their opinions in the time of Mary and had come into close contact with the Reformers of Geneva, Zürich, and Frankfort, who were not satisfied with this. They wished to go further in the way of destruction, and they created a strong body of opinion in favour of destruction. Their efforts were helped by the course of external politics. Queen Elizabeth was excommunicated by the Pope, and her life and throne were constantly plotted against by Papal emissaries. Our country was engaged in a life and death struggle with Spain, which culminated in the threatened invasion of the

went in the direction of Puritanism: ' They say that kneeling is not commanded in Scripture: and what is not commanded in Scripture is unlawful. *There is the root of the errors of the sects!* If that be true, take away the whole Book of Service ; and let us have no more trouble in setting forth an order in religion, or indeed in common policy' (quoted by Dixon, *Hist. of Ch. of Eng.*, iii. 476).

Spanish Armada. All this was traced to the machinations of Rome. And then at the beginning of the reign of James I there was the fresh excitement of Gunpowder Plot, followed at the end of the century by the short-lived tyranny of the Roman Catholic James II. What wonder if there sank deep into the heart of the English people a settled dread of Roman agencies and Roman ways! Hence it is that the cry of 'No Popery' has always been so popular. The distrust and dislike of Rome became a national tradition.

To this day that tradition has not wholly worked itself out. And yet it has been to a large extent unreasoning and ill-founded. The liberties of England are far too firmly planted to be in any real danger now. And if we try to cast away prejudice and look at things Roman with an open mind, it cannot I think be denied that we have done them much injustice. We have been so intent upon making out a case against Roman Catholicism that we have too often looked upon it at its worst instead of at its best. Should we ourselves bear to be judged upon these terms? If we try to find out what there is of good in our Roman fellow Christians, we certainly can find it. Think for a moment of the Sisters of Mercy whose very name is a proverb for devotion to the cause of suffering humanity. Think of Father Damien and his lepers, and of the host of Roman Catholic missionaries, exiles from their homes, who in numbers and in zeal emulate our own. Think of the saintly lives, of which from time to time we have glimpses, of many a humble curé in secluded Alpine valleys or by the storm-beaten shores of the Atlantic. Think of the bands of scholars in France and Belgium, in Germany and Italy, who are moved by a genuine love of knowledge and of truth, and who are seeking to spread both by all the means in their power. Where these things are we may be sure that the blessing of God is, and that the name of Christ is not invoked in vain.

There is many a loyal son of the Church of England, deeply attached to the Mother that bare him and proud of her history and of her characteristic excellences, who yet cannot help seeing that some virtues and graces have been more highly developed in the stock from which we have broken off than in that to which we belong.

If it is true, it is also right that we should feel thus. By so doing we are all the more likely to improve the inheritance which God has given us. And in any case the cultivation of such mutual understanding and sympathy must be the first step towards the reuniting of the scattered members of the Body of Christ.

That is a hope that we cannot and must not surrender. Our duty at the present time is to try to heal these old breaches and not to widen them. But I shall be told that the risk is great in adopting these ancient institutions which have certainly in the past been abused. Yes, there is a risk, which must be set against any possible profit, and may well justify caution and a tactful and elastic rule—leaving them to make their way on their own merits where they are congenial, and scrupulously abstaining from any attempt to force or obtrude them where they are not. We say that some of these institutions have been abused; but Why? Because they were not kept sweet and clean by the flowing through them of a stream of strong and deep and genuine Christianity. The great safeguard against all possible abuses, the one article of a standing or a falling Church, is the cultivation

of the spirit of Christ. Where there is a real
and intense loyalty to Him, there we may be
sure will be the fruits of the Spirit, which will
bud and blossom even through institutions that
are not without their dangers. And where this
is wanting we shall have a Church hard and
cold and lifeless, however careful it may be
to keep itself clear of contamination. Do not
let us be in haste to pluck the mote out of
the eye of our brother, but to pluck the beam
out of our own. We may be sure that the
best way even to advance the interests of
a party is to strengthen and deepen the hold
of that party upon Christ Himself and the
principles of Christ. And if we each and all
make this our aim, we shall find that insensibly
in drawing near to Christ we have drawn nearer
to each other, that we are really 'perfected
together in the same mind and in the same
judgement,' that we have really learnt to 'speak
the same thing.'

APPENDIX I

K

EPISCOPACY AND SACERDOTALISM

Dr. Moberly's Comments [1]

THE service which Dr. Sanday's work renders to controversy is beyond praise. Controversy indeed is itself an ineradicable necessity. It is a condition of progress towards clearness and towards unity of thought. Yet what is called the controversial spirit is a most unlovely thing. Based upon intellectual injustice—perhaps, even, intellectual incapacity of justice—it has found its characteristic methods in unfair exaggeration or hardly honest suppression, in telling sarcasm, or triumphant repartee.

Dr. Sanday's work is the precise contradictory of all this. Not only is it unfailing in temper and courtesy, it is also distinguished by that

---

[1] Reprinted from the *Guardian* of January 16, 1899, by permission of Dr. Moberly and the Editor.

K 2

rarest of rare gifts, a sincere intellectual generosity. The first impulse of most men is to
criticize even what they may ultimately be
driven, in greater or smaller measure, to accept.
Probably it is Dr. Sanday's first impulse to
accept with generosity even what, on reflection,
he may be compelled more or less seriously to
criticize. And so his attitude in criticizing, while
it is in delightful contrast with what is generally
thought to be the attitude of a controversialist,
is a lesson of the highest moral beauty and value
to those in all time who are called to take part
in controversy. Full unstinted justice, if not
more than justice, to those whose point of view
differs from his own—this is the characteristic
basis of his thought and work.

It does not, of course, follow from what has
been said that the results which he reaches are
always rightly balanced, nor even that his
admirable generosity of spirit is wholly without
a certain liability of its own towards inexactness
of result. Perhaps every excellence has its own
liability to defect, and in this case that liability
would take the form of a possibly undue acceptance at the same moment of various views
which are not quite really compatible. Such

tolerance, if it ever touches excess, would involve some consequent loss of the clear definiteness (not to say enthusiasm) of insight, which must probably be acknowledged to be characteristic of those, whether uninspired or inspired, who have seen, in fact, most deeply into truth. If there is a true extent, yet the extent is strictly limited, in which it can be said that the prophet, as prophet, sees truth in every imperfect form of statement. At least, if he sees truth clearly, he clearly sees untruth too.

Dr. Sanday has, in this volume, referred largely to a book of mine, and he has made it exceptionally easy for me to comment on what he has said, at once publicly and in my own name. The volume is quite plainly intended as an eirenicon. And there is much in every part of it which deserves the name. The first sermon is a contribution to the idea of 'the unity of the Church.' A sketch is given (pp. 7-9) of Dr. Hort's conception of unity, as to which I can only say that if this were the entire sum of what Dr. Hort said, I should hardly have found myself in the invidious position of criticizing Dr. Hort. To a great extent Dr. Sanday regards this sketch as harmonizing, or at least compatible, with the idea of unity in *Ministerial Priesthood.* Yet he feels that there is a difference, represented to him by the use, on the one side, of the phrase 'essential,' on the other, of the words 'dominant' and 'peremptory.' Perhaps Dr. Sanday sees more meaning in these latter words than they were intended to bear. They were intended to express the principle that maintenance, so far as is possible, of outward unity is not only a Christian aspiration, but a Christian *duty.* They meant that wilful breach of organized unity is to the conscience of an instructed Christian 'schism'; and that 'schism' is not only a mistake but a sin. But probably Dr. Sanday himself says as much as this—in his own name and in Dr. Hort's. Thus (p. 14) :—

'He, too, would say that this transcendental unity cannot be only transcendental. It is, and it must be, continually realizing itself in the Church upon earth. No Christian, and no society of Christians, can escape the pressing duty of making the unity which exists in name more and more real and vital. Let us lay down all this in the strongest terms possible.'

Does the 'pressing duty' here spoken of forbid the overt setting up of rival congregations and rival altars in a community, as well as the suspicion and intolerance of inward feeling? If it does, there is indeed little difference between the two views, as Dr. Sanday states them.

But, of course, no statement of the principle of unity, whether as 'essential' or as 'peremptory,' will settle details in the application of the principle. There will still remain such questions as Dr. Sanday asks (p 14). The question as to the relation of uniformity to unity will mean, in fact, in this context, the question (itself primarily historical) as to (*a*) the indispensableness, (*b*) the adequacy of the system of Episcopacy. No one, for instance, would suppose that if, in a divine mood of mutual penitence, the Greek Church and the Roman and the Anglican were to embrace each other in full communion, it would be indispensable for unity that their differently organized systems should be otherwise amalgamated; or that, if the Church of England and the Kirk of Scotland were prepared to unite, there would be any other serious question of organization *except* that of Episcopal orders and oversight. The parallels, therefore, to which Dr. Sanday points, to show that unity is not simple uniformity, are instructive and helpful.

His second question is as to 'the exact nature of the obligation' which the 'pressing duty' of making unity real and vital imposes; and the 'exact place of this duty in the scale of Christian duties generally.' To the statement of this question I can take no exception whatever. And if I could not admit that the Scripture leaves us with 'not a word' touching 'uniformity of outward organization,' I should certainly agree that, subject to the limitation of a few great principles, Christian uniformity is compatible with great and elastic possibilities of difference.

It belongs, perhaps, to Dr. Sanday's instinctive generosity to an antagonist that the next pages are largely occupied with an apology for the separations and separatists of the sixteenth century, not on the ground that they were right, but on the ground that the greatest allowances are to be made for the circumstances under which they went wrong. It is good for us to learn to feel not sympathy only, but hearty gratitude, for every word which is urged upon us in this sense. The last fifteen pages, therefore, of the sermon deserve the most careful attention.

I should like to make one comment more before leaving it. On the second page Dr. Sanday explains that the two principles or methods which his opening words refer to are practically inseparable. Neither is ever completely without the other. If, then, both are necessary parts or aspects of the interpretation of 'the doctrine and institutions of the New Testament' (as they are, and are made to be on page 2), is it not a little hard to begin on page 1 by suggesting that while one of the two has a recognized method and *status*, it is doubtful whether the other has a right to either? Could any one read Dr. Sanday's first paragraph sympathetically without feeling that the second of the two methods was already not a little discredited?

But, in fact, what he calls the historical or (in some sort) inductive method, whilst it would be the only method reasonably possible to a wholly impartial intellect from Japan or Thibet, cannot—as he goes on, in a measure, to allow —be the whole of the interpretative method of a Christian student. A Christian student who would understand the full force of some emphatic utterance of our Lord, or the significance of distinctive Christian institutions, must ultimately see them as consequences outflowing from the doctrine of the Incarnation—as particulars in that universal—as parts in that whole. He may do his best to examine them first of all as an inquirer from outside might examine them, and so to see what meaning they would yield in detachment from the Christian hypothesis, and, therefore, how far they can be said, from their *quasi*-independent position, to confirm or to modify the statement of that hypothesis. But whether it be such a solemn asseveration as ' I am the Resurrection and the Life,' or whether it be the significance of (say) the laying on of hands in Acts viii, his understanding of them must be necessarily still incomplete—still, more or less, in the tentative stage, which is natural to the man whose mind is not yet on the great issue fully made up—until they are parts to him of his belief in ' the Son ' and ' the Holy Ghost,' and the whole meaning of his belief in ' the Son ' and ' the Holy Ghost' enters into and lights up his understanding of them.

I cannot, therefore, but gently protest against a mode of opening statement which will generally (as I fear) be understood to imply that the interpretation of such passages or incidents from the neutral platform of the outsider is scientific or regular, while that which is based upon the insight of the insider can but offer doubtful apologies in its own defence.

The second sermon raises the question of the origin of the ministry, whether it was, in principle, 'evolved' out of the conditions and inherent powers of the Church, or 'devolved' by and from Apostolic authority—if, indeed, there was strictly such a thing as Apostolic authority at all. Dr. Hort's denial of any formal Apostolic authority is discussed with (at least) much sympathy of tone. Nevertheless, I must submit that upon Dr. Sanday's own statement as a whole (pp. 42-53) the conclusion ought certainly to be adverse to Dr. Hort. And if this statement were supplemented by section 2 of the first address in Dr. Bright's *Aspects of Primitive Church Life* (pp. 12-26), that conclusion would be very considerably emphasized.

But the crucial question in respect of this part of Dr. Sanday's argument is—What is meant by 'evolution'? He has insisted (p. 40) that the word in any case must mean a development intended and directed by the providence of God. And when we come to p. 54 it appears that evolution is not an alternative to devolution at all. It is not intended to *deny* the principle of

Apostolic transmission, only to insist that there were steps in the development of the Christian ministry, and that these steps had their own natural occasion and history in the developing circumstances of the Church.   Thus it is a most notable fact that the appointment of the Seven in Acts vi. is quoted as 'an exact example' of what Dr. Sanday 'understands by evolution' (p. 54).   But this appointment, whilst growing out of the politic conditions, and emphasizing the corporate action, of the Church, includes also, and no less emphatically, the distinctive action of the appointing Apostles.   Dr. Sanday's words are :—

'The initiative comes from them, and certain parts of the formal appointment are discharged by them—whether claimed by them as a right or spontaneously left to them by the Church does not appear.'

In reference to the adequacy of this description cf. also Dr. Bright's *Aspects*, p. 21 and note.   If this 'exactly' represents what is meant by those who contend for an evolutionary origin of the ministry, there is nothing whatever with which the champions of devolution need quarrel.   They have only to maintain the significance of their own side of a process which is admitted to be two-sided. It is much to be hoped, then, that Dr. Sanday's discussion of evolution and devolution may help towards a real combination of what is meant on both sides.

And so, in respect of Episcopacy (pp. 60-64), we certainly need not hesitate to agree that there was an aspect in which, had we lived (say) from A. D. 60-130, we should have seen the ' gradual ' and ' natural ' consolidation of Episcopacy. We demur to this only so far as it is erected into a dogmatic principle, for the purpose of denying the Church's belief in a ministry transmitted from the beginning.

The remaining pages of the sermon plead for the recognition of God's work in various bodies which have (whether more or less excusably) abandoned the historic basis of Church ministry. We recognize it in all reverence, unhesitatingly and unstintingly. But such a recognition is wholly compatible with an assured belief that their act in abandoning the historic organization of the Church was itself definitely wrong.

Appended to this sermon is a quotation from *Clem. Rom.* xliv. It is given with great care, in Greek and Latin and English. It is given, moreover, as 'the passage' of this Epistle which bears upon the question of Apostolic Succession. Now, I cannot help thinking that, in offering this limited quotation, Dr. Sanday (like the authors of an article on 'Apostolical Succession' in the *Contemporary Review* for August, 1898) does very imperfect justice to the appeal to St. Clement. As the matter is of considerable importance, I have ventured to offer again a shortened paraphrase of the argument, not in the forty-fourth chapter only, but from the thirty-seventh onward, premising only that for this purpose I have not hesitated to lay more emphasis upon some points in the thought than they obviously bear in the context as a whole, though I do not believe that I have really exaggerated the argument in any particular. Clement says, then :—

'Consider the Roman army—its coherence through distinction of offices--its unity through subordination. Under the supremacy of the Emperor and his generals, there are captains of thousands, and of hundreds, and of fifties, and so to the end. Soldiers cannot all be tribunes or centurions; but men and officers equally need each other; and unity is the due mutual relation of all. So it is with the members of the human body. And so in the Church, mutual subordination is the principle of the life of the body. All alike, though diversely endowed and empowered, have need of each other. By this mutual relation—each in the place which God has assigned to him—do we glorify God. It is the merest folly if men lift themselves up against conditions like these.

'Is it not manifest that obedience to our Master requires this submission to order? Nothing is random or accidental in His service. There are places, and times, and persons determined by Him; and acceptance with Him depends on observance of these. In the old covenant the high priests, the priests, the Levites, the lay people had each their own place assigned. And so in the Christian worship each must keep his appointed place. If such distinctions were peremptory under the law, and the penalty of transgression was death, how much deeper the necessity with us! The fuller our spiritual insight, so much the greater our peril if we transgress!

'So then it is with the ministry of the Church. The Apostles were charged with the gospel by Jesus Christ. Jesus Christ was sent from God. Christ, then, from God; the Apostles from Christ; and the Apostles, in their turn, made bishops and deacons of the best of their converts. This is the principle of order by the will of God.

'So in the Old Testament, Moses, himself the "faithful servant in the whole house," was followed and confirmed by all later prophets. And as in the Old Testament Moses vindicated to the tribe of Aaron the exclusive right of priesthood, as a right of Divine appointment, through a miracle (the issue of which miracle he himself foresaw, but which was meant to preclude all future possibility of jealous questioning); so the Apostles ordered things as they did as a result of inspired fore-knowledge, because they, too, foresaw that the office of rule over the Christian flock would come otherwise into dispute. To preclude, then, all doubt or questioning, they first themselves ordained their best converts to ministry, and provided further that, as vacancies arose, others should receive the same ministry by succession from these. And since this is the basis of Christian office, it is more than an error, it is a grievous sin, to displace those whose title to presbyterate is their appointment—in the face, and with the voice, of the whole Church—whether by the Apostles themselves, or by other elect brethren after the Apostles.'

It seems to me quite a misreading of the argument of this passage to suppose that the emphasis can be laid upon the 'consentient voice of the whole Church' (however important that may be in its own way), or upon the maintenance only of constituted office, without reference to the basis of principle upon which that constitution to office depends. It seems to me that the whole argument turns upon the principle of devolution, through Apostles, from Christ and from God; and that there is simply no trace whatever, and no room for the insertion, of what Dr. Bright calls the 'democratic' basis of ministry. And I must add that, considering the force and clearness of the general principle thus argued for, it seems to me inconsistent with an adequate appreciation of the passage as a whole, to fasten, upon the possible ambiguity of the final phrase, a suggestion that the 'other elect brethren' (or 'other eminent men') may have been themselves outside the continuity of Apostolic devolution. Verbally, of the phrase by itself, this is possible enough. But I must submit that the phrase, if so interpreted, would precisely contradict and destroy the entire tenour of the argument at the close of which it stands.

But, after all, the first two sermons, with the questions which they help to raise, or help to determine, are, in character, preliminary. It is the third sermon which gives its title to the book; and, even apart from such an indication, it is easy to recognize that it is the third sermon which represents the most solemn climax of the writer's effort. The subject of the third is 'sacerdotalism.' Dr. Sanday takes this word as indicating the line of 'deepest cleavage' in the Church of England. But he attempts to show that even this 'deepest cleavage' is in large measure an unnecessary cleavage, the result rather of mutual misunderstanding than of essential antithesis. This he does by looking 'full in the face' the very thing which 'sacerdotalists' really mean; and finding that it represents, on ultimate analysis, an aspect of Christian truth. In its candour, and in its earnestness, this utterance upon sacerdotalism is singularly impressive. It is difficult not to nurse the hope that its eirenic character may prove to be of permanent importance.

Within the first three pages he implies the belief that the larger part of the really constitutive Eucharistic doctrine—on the one hand, of Bishop Lightfoot, when he denounces 'sacerdotalism,' and, on the other hand, of *Ministerial Priesthood* which defends it—is substantially one and the same. For my own part, I have often had pleasure in the avowal that my own *positive* Eucharistic meaning would (as I believe) differ very little, if it really would differ at all, from that of Bishop Lightfoot. But this is eminently a matter in which thought, in the long run, is apt to conform itself to words, and, therefore, words are of paramount importance. Dr. Sanday neither denies this nor emphasizes it. He raises (on p. 79) the question by what canon we are to determine the true import of words. The question is both important and difficult. For, in fact, the deeper the significance of any word the less adequate is any general canon of inter-pretative method. In the case of the deepest (which are also the most complex) conceptions of all, words at their best are but efforts towards a meaning which transcends them still. It was a piece of shallow play, very irritating in such a writer as Mr. Matthew Arnold, to appear to hunt out what Theists meant by God by etymo-logical experiments upon the familiar versions of His name. In words of very little signifi-cance this method may be useful. Yet to find what Christians mean by sin, or grace, or forgiveness, or spirit, or God, by tracing the verbal origin of the terms, would be worse than use-less.   Once for all Christianity read undreamt-of depths of meaning into old words.   And, more than this, every step in true Christian insight brings for the individual Christian fresh signifi-cance into words which, as words, were entirely familiar before.

Bishop Lightfoot finds, in Old Testament conceptions, the standard of the meaning of the word 'sacrifice.'   Upon this Dr. Sanday says (p. 80) :—

'A process so exceedingly natural, so broadly intelligible, so directly in touch with the instincts of the plain man cannot be otherwise than legitimate.'

We may admit that the process is 'natural.' But is it, therefore, 'legitimate'?   Perhaps yes, if what is meant is that 'the plain man' cannot, without some pedantry, be always censured for so using the word in ordinary contexts.   But surely no, if such a canon of interpretation is laid down by a theologian for the purpose of condemning as wrong the immemorial language and meaning of the Catholic Church in the region of her deepest experience.   It is no question of casual conversation for collateral purposes. The question is seriously raised— What is, from the point of view of Christian theology, the real and true meaning of the word 'sacrifice'? Under such conditions I would ask, with all seriousness, can we, without consciously adopting a principle so inadequate that it *must* mislead into confusion and error, go back upon the etymological, or the primitive, or the Mosaic, or any other conception of the content of the word, except that which our deepening Christian insight teaches us to discern in the one only true and absolute sacrifice, which is the sacrifice of Jesus Christ? Can we, with our eyes opening to the one perfect meaning, really say that other preliminary and imperfect meanings are, not merely pardonable in current language, but tenable as the basis of theological definition and theological condemnation? If not, then even whilst (or, indeed, even *because*) I may feel that my positive Eucharistic meaning is really very near to Bishop Lightfoot's, I must still hold myself not entitled only, but bound, so far as this most important word is concerned, not so much to plead that the bishop, though impugning it, is right, as to protest that, in impugning it, he is perilously wrong.

Whilst expressing my gratitude for the pages which follow, may I suggest that, when Dr. Sanday says (p. 83) that the Christian—

'must do all this not in his own strength but in the strength of Christ, on whom his affections are so concentrated that it is as if Christ and he were actually one,'

there is in his sentence one un-Scriptural touch? The un-Scriptural touch is in the insertion of the words 'as if.' This is hardly the occasion for enlarging upon the thoughts involved in this point. But I may express my belief that the main effort of Christian theological exposition, on more topics than one, will for some time have to lie in the direction of showing that no 'as if,' in a context like this, is needed to make Scripture language either intelligible or real. And the more deeply this truth is realized, the less (I cannot but fancy) will the distinction between sacrificing and pleading or presenting a sacrifice, suggested by Dr. Sanday (p. 86) as 'inexpugnable,' be felt to be a substantial or ultimate distinction. The words which he quotes with praise, 'He pleads by what He is,' will more and more be found to have an application, as primarily to Christ, so both to the corporate Church, which is His Body, and also to the Christian individual, who only finds at last his true self in the consummation of his oneness with Christ.

But it may be that there is something invidious in calling attention to points of criticism at all. For indeed the sermon is a great, a solemn, and a very generous effort—an effort for truth, and for the unity which is based not upon superficial compromise, but upon deepening insight into truth. I, at least, cannot but thankfully rejoice when, writing in such a spirit, Dr. Sanday finds himself able substantially to accept, in his own name and in that of Bishop Lightfoot, the exposition offered in *Ministerial Priesthood*, and with it the immemorial terminology of priestliness and sacrifice in Christ's Church, as being essentially true and characteristically Christian. If in so doing he would none the less strenuously combat the materialisms and the arrogances which are the besetting sins of a false sacerdotalism, real believers in the priestly Church should be the foremost to show that such a strenuousness is a necessary part of their own battle for truth.

It may possibly seem to some readers as if a more direct emphasis were laid on the largely metaphorical language of Rom. xv. 15, 16 (it is the text of the sermon, and see p. 89) than Dr. Sanday would himself probably intend. Of course, St. Paul is not there directly describing the Christian ministry as sacerdotal; much less explaining or enjoining sacerdotal phraseology. The passage is indeed of importance for the purpose. But it is just its incidental and allusive character which gives it its special force. Another point should perhaps be mentioned, though it is a minute one. Verbally, then, I should hardly myself (at least without careful distinction) have quite used the phrase (on p. 92) 'is no priesthood at all.'

On the other hand, I would draw most respectful attention to what is said (on p. 98) about Nonconformists and Episcopacy; only borrowing, while I do so, Dr. Sanday's own words in a somewhat different context :—

'If I may say so, I regard these protests as of especial value, because they come from quarters from which advice and remonstrance will be listened to. It is better for those of us who can speak with less of sympathy to keep silent.'

It is perhaps natural that every one should think his own thought eirenic. If I am to confess that this was so with me, and that it was a matter of some disappointment at first that comments, especially upon the Evangelical side of thought, showed but little sign even of suspecting such a purpose or such a possibility in my work, it is, indeed, far more than a compensation to have been met with such large generosity, not to say so much deep reality of agreement, by a writer like Dr. Sanday—a writer who, starting antecedently (as he says) from a point of view widely different from my own, and never merging either the candid critic in the kind friend or the kind friend in the candid critic, yet reaches conclusions which contain so much promise of mutual understanding. To me at least, if I may venture to say so, the things which he has said with such impressive earnestness are as the breath of a great refreshment, rich with present encouragement and rare largeness of future hope.

The fourth sermon in the volume is no less characteristic of Dr. Sanday's temper of mind and spirit.   But its topic is somewhat different, and it has already been commented on in the *Guardian*.   Of it I would only say that the outlook upon Church prospects which is the most sanguine—because the most charitable, and the most immovably rooted in faith and hope —can be rarely, if ever, very deeply mistaken.

APPENDIX II

EPISCOPACY AND SACERDOTALISM

REPLY TO DR. MOBERLY[1]

SOME weeks ago there appeared in the *Guardian* under this heading what I may call a review of my little book, *The Conception of Priesthood*, by my friend and colleague Dr. Moberly. Regarded as a review, nothing could have been more kind and generous ; but I am quite aware that my book received the consideration it did chiefly because it was in the main an attempt to bring the two sides in some of the leading controversies of our day nearer together. It is very true that it aimed at this, and I am deeply indebted to Dr. Moberly for his help in carrying the process (as I hope it may be carried) a step further.

It would not become me to speak of the opening paragraphs in which, like a friend rather than a critic, he characterizes my personal share

[1] Reprinted from the *Guardian* of March 29, 1899, by permission of the Editor.

in the controversy. The intention, at least, has
been what he gives it credit for being, whatever
may have been the shortcomings in execution.
But I should like to clear myself of one heresy
to which the particular line that I have taken and
the temper ascribed to me might be thought
liable. I do not in the least believe that truth
lies in compromises; or that real differences can
be glossed over by ambiguities of language. If
anything that I have written should seem to
give evidence of this delusion the fault must be
in some want of clearness of statement or of
perception; it is not a fault of principle. To
clear myself on this head is not to say that there
are not in my mind many things that are opposite,
and some—perhaps not a few—that are incompatible. The seeker after truth is constantly
discovering that his denials have been too sweeping, and that the adversary has positions and
arguments as good as his own. It is just this
which constitutes the infinite variety and com-
plexity of the world we live in. If all truth were
on one side things would be very much more of
a colour. But no sooner is the discovery made
that some of our negations are untenable than
the question arises how the opposing propositions

are to be adjusted to each other, how much of truth and how much of error there is in each. This is a life-long process ; a large part of what we mean by advance in knowledge consists in nothing else. And it seems to me that there is great danger in supposing that different principles are incompatible before they have been fully tested. The wolf and the lamb cannot lie down permanently together ; but all the occupants of our fields are not either wolves or lambs.

Another disclaimer that I should like to make has reference to the comparison with which my book began, of the two opposing methods which for want of better names I may call the historical or inductive, and the logical or deductive. Dr. Moberly thinks I did less than justice to the second of these, and that my words might even be taken to question its right to exist. I should be extremely sorry if this were so, and it was very far from my intention. I desired to hold the scales as evenly as I could.

But shall I say what is the real fact as to my own relation to the two methods ? This is just one of the instances in which I have discovered, late in the day, that an old prejudice was not as well founded as I thought. As far back as I can remember, even before I came up to Oxford, a deep impression was made upon me by Butler's *Analogy.* One fixed conclusion that I carried away with me from that work was that deductive arguments in the sphere of theology were highly precarious ; that our real concern was not with what *ought* to be, or what *must* be, in the Divine economy, but rather with what *is*, or, in the historical sense, what *has been.* This naturally led up to the use of the so-called historical method, which in these days enjoys much favour; and, to the extent of my ability, I have spent most of my life in trying to apply it.

But in the last year or two, since I came to know Dr. Moberly, I have become aware that the opposite method has a larger and more legitimate function than I had supposed. As wielded by him, I can see that it is an engine of great power ; and I have no wish to question its validity. He will, however, perhaps, allow me to say that I regard it still somewhat in the light of the 'bow of Ulysses.' Ulysses himself, I know, can bend and use it ; but I am not so sure of the other inhabitants of Ithaca. I will not prejudge them ; but I should like to see them try their skill before expressing an opinion.

Perhaps it may be possible to formulate a more exact definition of the spheres of the two methods; but I cannot say that I have done this at present.

The first of the discourses criticized by Dr. Moberly was on the Unity of the Church as the underlying principle of the organized society. In regard to this, I am glad to think that we are practically agreed. I had taken exception to some expressions of Dr. Moberly's, not so much in themselves as because of the use which I feared might be made of them. He explains, however, that they were intended to assert—

'The principle that maintenance, so far as possible, of outward unity is not only a Christian aspiration but a Christian duty. They meant that wilful breach of organized unity is to the conscience of an instructed Christian "schism," and that "schism" is not only a mistake but a sin.'

This I can endorse—in the abstract and as a law for one's own conscience. But when it came to applying it to the concrete as a principle of historical judgement, I feel sure that Dr. Moberly would agree with me that the greatest circumspection would be needed. A multitude of questions would arise which would have to be considered before a verdict could be given.   I doubt whether any of the greater divisions among Christians could be called exactly 'wilful.'   I should like to quote in this connexion a letter that I have received from a Nonconformist friend:—

'I thought,' he writes, 'that while you were just to the Reformers as leaders of a moral revolt, you were something less than just in holding them to such an extent responsible for the breaking up of the Unity of Western Christendom.   They were here most unwilling authors of division; it was Rome that refused all terms, and sharpened her own antitheses.   If you compare, e. g., the Decrees and Canons of Trent with the Confession of Augsburg or the *Helvetica*, both the *Prior* and the *Posterior*, you will be struck with the eirenical character of the Protestant Confessions and the polemical temper of the Roman.   In the one case there were materials for a discussion which might have achieved unity; in the other exclusion of all who did not accept the newly formulated dogmas of the Roman Church.   And certainly it is the party which presents an *ultimatum* consisting for the most part of doctrines before unformulated, and demands for it unqualified acceptance, that may be justly regarded as the author of division.'

I believe there is much truth in this, though, perhaps, it would not be right to lay too much stress on the fact simply that the doctrines in question were unformulated. On that ground we know that the Arians complained of the decision at Nicaea. But, speaking broadly, it seems to me very true that the Reformers did not court disruption, but found themselves involved in it against their will and in prosecuting what we can see to have been to a large extent righteous causes. This, for instance, is the heading with which the so-called *Confessio Saxonica* of 1551 was issued:—*Confessio Doctrinae Saxonicarum Ecclesiarum Synodo Tridentinae oblata,* Anno Domini MDLI: *in qua, Christiane lector, videbis, quinam e Catholicae Ecclesiae gremio resilierunt; et per quos stet, quo minus Ecclesiae pia concordia sarciatur.*

On the whole of this subject I do not doubt that Dr. Moberly would be as ready to join hands with me on my side of the proposition as I should be to join hands with him on his. On the next step, the origin of the ministry, the interval between us would, I am afraid, still be rather wider. Not that I can say that I was satisfied with my own treatment of the subject, or that I for a moment suppose myself to have spoken the last word in regard to it. Just for this reason I hesitate now to express, and even to form, a decided opinion on it. The inquiry into the origin of the Christian ministry is one of international scope; it is in the hands of many scholars at once, who are making their way painfully by inches through an obscure and difficult problem. My own place in this body of students is not a prominent one, and at the present moment I should prefer to wait for my colleagues.

In regard to the antithesis of 'evolution' or 'devolution,' I understand that a large part of what I should be interested to affirm Dr. Moberly would not deny. His theory has room for the only kind of evolution that I should care to claim. · On the other hand, I should be equally willing to accept so much of devolution as can be historically proved. Not only we, but I imagine all Christians would be agreed that the ultimate authorization for ministry comes from God. The only question would be as to the precise channel through which that authorization was conveyed.

I am not at all concerned to deny that from

the end of the second century onwards a certain mode of conveyance has been regular. I do not doubt that even before that date a similar mode had been practised—and we might even, perhaps, say regularly practised—but with what degree of regularity, and how far back that regularity extended, the evidence does not permit us to determine. I also do not doubt that this mode of conveyance, like other parts of the established ecclesiastical order, has been attended by its appropriate blessing.

But I am not prepared so to erect it into a law of the Divine action as to say that there is no blessing conveyed by any other. I believe that the rule which Dr. Moberly lays down is too stringent and too *a priori*; and I am glad to think that it is so, not because I wish to question its positive side, but because it has also a negative side which is turned against those who have deviated from the ecclesiastical order. I think that I enjoy some advantages which they do not, but I should hesitate to say that their ministry has not a validity of its own.

The points on which Dr. Moberly's impressive work, *Ministerial Priesthood*, seemed to me most open to question were in regard to prophecy and the literature relating to prophecy. I could not at all accept his estimate of the evidence supplied by the *Didaché*. Both on external and on internal grounds I must needs attach to it considerably more importance than he does. And I regard the prophetic gift as something far more co-ordinate with (and in the Apostolic age superior to) the local ministry than subordinate to it. I conceive that we are right in interpreting prophecy in the New Testament on the full analogy of prophecy in the Old. The prophet by the side of the [presbyter-] bishop and deacon in the *Didaché* seems to me to correspond almost exactly to the Old Testament prophet by the side of the priest. A priest might also be a prophet, just as a presbyter might also be a prophet, but there was no necessary connexion between the two. And the prophet, if I am not mistaken, represented a different and alternative principle.

The presence of this other principle seems to me to make the Providential ordering of things easier to understand. I am not prepared to put the prophets of later ages quite on the same level with the Biblical prophets, but I do not think that the gift has wholly died out. We seem to need something of the kind to explain certain phenomena, not only in Christianity, but in some non-Christian religions. They may be irregular, but they are not therefore χωρὶς Θεοῦ.

Another question which goes to the root of the matter is that as to the significance of the laying-on of hands. It is, no doubt, a wide-spread idea that this denotes *transmission*—the transmission of a property possessed by one person to another. But it cannot really mean this. It is a common accompaniment of 'blessing'— i. e., of the invoking of blessing. It is God who blesses or bestows the gift; and it is in no way implied that the gift is previously possessed by him who invokes it. True, that 'the less is blessed of the greater'; but that does not mean that the greater *imparts* a blessing. When we come to think of this, it seems clear enough; and the inference suggested is one for which we may be thankful. It may save us from some mechanical and unworthy ways of conceiving historic con-tinuity, which is just as real without them.

On the group of questions connected with the origin of Episcopacy there is much that must still remain open; such approximation as has been made is incomplete. But on the other fundamental question, the validity of the conception which lies behind what is called 'sacerdotalism,' I must needs profess myself satisfied. On this I do not feel that I have any substantial contro-versy with Dr. Moberly. We are concerned far more with the discussions of the future than with those of the past; and I firmly believe that if in future disputants are careful to state precisely in what sense they affirm or deny the sacrificial aspect of the Christian priesthood, they will soon come to find that they are nearer to each other than they had supposed.

It is true that there is one profound subject on which Dr. Moberly uses different language from mine; and true also that my own words were deliberately chosen. The difference here is real and important; but I cannot regard it as matter for controversy. I had said that the Christian must 'die to sin' and 'put off the old man,' and that 'he must do all this, not in his own strength, but in the strength of Christ, on whom his affections are so concentrated that it is as if Christ and he were actually one.'

On this Dr. Moberly remarks that there is in my sentence one un-Scriptural touch:—

'The un-Scriptural touch is in the insertion of

the words "as if." This is hardly the occasion for enlarging upon the thoughts involved in this point. But I may express my belief that the main effort of Christian theological exposition, on more topics than one, will for some time have to lie in the direction of showing that no "as if," in a context like this, is needed to make Scripture language either intelligible or real. And the more deeply the truth is realized, the less (I cannot but fancy) will the distinction between sacrificing and pleading or presenting a sacrifice, suggested by Dr. Sanday as "inexpugnable," be felt to be a substantial or ultimate distinction.'

The whole of this paragraph is deeply interesting to me, and I suspect that it will be to not a few besides. I greatly hope that it may not be long before Dr. Moberly finds an opportunity to explain his meaning more fully. I look back upon a time when the words 'as if,' to which he objects, came to me as the solution of a problem by which I had been much perplexed. I had asked myself, What is the meaning of the strong language about union with Christ which we find in St. Paul's Epistles, and notably in Romans vi. ? How are we to translate it into terms of our own experience ? I argued thus : Actual union it cannot mean, because that would imply a fusion of personalities, and fusion of personalities is impossible. If there is one thing that personality means, it is distinctness. I am myself and no one else. But what is the nearest thing in human experience to the fusion of per-sonalities? I answered—and here I thought that I had found the key to St. Paul's language —Surely it must be in the life of affection, when—

> heart with heart in concord beats,
> And the lover is beloved.

The most effective way of getting rid of selfish-ness and self-will is through some overpower-ing attachment. There, at last, you may have two wills really acting as one. On that analogy I could explain and make real to myself the seemingly mystical language of St. Paul. His great moral leverage is the attachment of the Christian to Christ. That is at bottom what he means by *faith*.

This was the kind of process that I went through with myself some fifteen years ago. I reached that point which seemed to me—and has since seemed—fairly satisfactory. But if Dr. Moberly has something better to offer, I keep an open mind and shall be grateful for instruction. A good many indications seem to point to the conclusion that the thought of our time is preparing itself for a further advance on this subject. I have never seen my own view tested by really penetrating criticism. Its great advantage has seemed to me that it is at least real as far as it goes. But I would not say that it is not possible to go further.

For the rest I am glad to think that Dr. Moberly and I can stand (from our somewhat different points of view) shoulder to shoulder. I am not in the least surprised to find myself told, from both extremities of the scale, in tones friendly but decided, that the eirenicon which Dr. Moberly had proposed, and which I have defended, cannot be accepted. A Roman Catholic reviewer contends that we are 'seeking peace through a confusion rather than through a clearer statement of contrary beliefs'; that we endeavour 'to substitute an academically defensible and philosophical sense of the word "sacrifice" for that which it actually bears in the usage of the belligerents.' And on the other hand the *Christian World* assures me that—

'The difference between Sacerdotalism and its opponents is vital. It is a question on which sides must be taken, and to satisfactorily face it one must sometimes be controversial.'

Even the editor of the *Expository Times*, who evidently goes with me as far as he possibly can, thinks that on this point of hottest conflict the attempt to draw the two sides nearer together has completely failed.

It would be ungrateful not to recognize that there are exceptions to this verdict from some who are themselves inclined to favour the middle view. But, broadly speaking, it must be confessed that neither Dr. Moberly nor I have succeeded in making an impression where we should most like to make it. I would, however, earnestly entreat the 'belligerents' on both sides—I will not say to attend to us, but to reconsider the question for themselves on its merits once more. All who are engaged in the controversy are Christians ; all those with whom I am at present concerned agree in celebrating the Eucharistic feast; the great majority also agree in entrusting the lead in that celebration to ministers specially set apart for that purpose. Nearly all, again, would agree in describing the death of the Lord Jesus Christ upon Calvary as a sacrifice; and nearly all

would regard the Eucharist as in intimate relation to that Death, which they allow to be
sacrificial. The heart of the controversy lies
in the one question, *What* relation, and *what
share* in the relation, is borne by the ministers as
distinct from the people ? I still am not shaken
in my belief that if both sides in the controversy
would only set out in full and exact terms their
answer to these two questions, they would find
that, with their will or against it, they approach
more nearly to each other's position than while
they looked at it from a distance they had
imagined. We may be sure that the Great
Head of the Church does not mean His children to remain for ever in a deadlock ; and the
first step towards extricating themselves from it
does not lie in disguising their meaning, but in
determining with the utmost possible precision
what they mean.

A few words should, perhaps, be added on
the appeal to Scripture. The friend whom I
have quoted above writes as follows :—

'It seems to me as if the manifestly careful
abstention on the part of Jesus and of the Apostolic writers from the use of ἱερεύς for the
Christian, and the use of sacrificial terms like

θυσία in a strictly changed or figurative sense (Rom. xii. 1 ; Phil. ii. 17, where θυσία and λειτουργία have experienced a parallel transformation, iv. 18; Heb. xiii. 15, 16; 1 Pet. ii. 5), signified that they were specially anxious to avoid everything that could suggest the perpetuation of sacrificial offices, customs, and ideas of the Temple. . . . Take "priesthood" from the title of Canon Moberly's book, and it would lose its very *raison d'être* ; add ἱερωσύνη to Paul's conception of the ministry, and it would be essentially changed.'

I do not think that we can say as much as that. It is not indeed St. Paul, but a writer nearly akin to him, who says—'The priesthood being changed (μετατιθεμένης τῆς ἱερωσύνης), there is made of necessity a change also of the law' (Heb. vii. 12). But this seems to imply that the priesthood is only changed, and not abolished. And St. Paul uses θυσία expressly of the sacrifice of Christ (Eph. v. 2); he also uses sacrificial language expressly in connexion with the Eucharist (1 Cor. x. 18). When the solemn 'breaking of bread' is described, as in Acts xx. 11, xxvii. 35, the Christian will hardly say that the action is merely that of the ordinary Jewish housefather ; it has contracted new associations, through its symbolical connexion with the Body 'broken' upon the Cross (1 Cor. xi. 24 *v.l.*); and these associations are distinctly sacrificial.

The figurative use of language relating to sacrifice cannot be held to prove that sacrifice in any more substantial sense was discarded. There was an obvious and simple reason for it in the fact that the Temple system was still in full vigour. A perfectly literal use of ἱερεύς or θυσία was for the Christian impossible.

We must remember, further, that the Christian ministry, though in process of being constituted, had not yet assumed all its functions. Its functions were at least not consolidated as they were by the middle of the second century. We are still in the state of things represented by the *Didaché*, when the natural person to take the lead in the celebration of the Eucharist was the apostle or prophet, and when it was only in default of these that it fell to the officers of the local Church. Vague terms like ὁ προεστώς, ὁ προϊστάμενος were to be expected under such circumstances.

But if the usage of the New Testament favours the continuance of a definitely Christian idea of sacrifice, the usage of the early Church, from the *Didaché* and Justin onwards, is continuous and unequivocal. This usage is the main justification of views such as those expressed by Dr. Moberly. I cannot see how those who profess to give weight to primitive practice can take exception to them.

I think that my friend will understand the differences that still remain between us. He will see that their motive is not any obstinate refusal of proffered light. I desire to receive whatever shall ultimately prove to be true in history and true in doctrine. But I do not think it an improper bias to lean, as long as one can, to that interpretation both of history and of doctrine which enables us to embrace the greatest number of facts, and to take a milder view of existing divisions.

OXFORD: HORACE HART
PRINTER TO THE UNIVERSITY

April 1899.

A Selection of Works

IN

THEOLOGICAL LITERATURE

PUBLISHED BY

Messrs. LONGMANS, GREEN, & CO.

London : 39 Paternoster Row, E.C.
New York : 91 and 93 Fifth Avenue.
Bombay : 32 Hornby Road.

Abbey and Overton.—THE ENGLISH CHURCH IN THE EIGHTEENTH CENTURY. By Charles J. Abbey, M.A., Rector of Checkendon, Reading, and John H. Overton, D.D., Canon of Lincoln. *Crown 8vo. 7s. 6d.*

Adams.—SACRED ALLEGORIES. The Shadow of the Cross —The Distant Hills—The Old Man's Home—The King's Messengers. By the Rev. William Adams, M.A. *Crown 8vo. 3s. 6d.*
    The four Allegories may be had separately, with Illustrations. *16mo. 1s. each.*

Aids to the Inner Life.
    Edited by the Venble. W. H. Hutchings, M.A., Archdeacon of Cleveland, Canon of York, Rector of Kirby Misperton, and Rural Dean of Malton. *Five Vols. 32mo, cloth limp, 6d. each; or cloth extra, 1s. each.*
    OF THE IMITATION OF CHRIST. By Thomas à Kempis.
    THE CHRISTIAN YEAR
    THE DEVOUT LIFE. By St. Francis de Sales.
    THE HIDDEN LIFE OF THE SOUL.
    THE SPIRITUAL COMBAT. By Laurence Scupoli.

Alexander.—THE CHRISTIANITY OF ST. PAUL. By the Rev. S. A. Alexander, M.A., Reader of the Temple Church.

Barnett.—THE SERVICE OF GOD : Sermons, Essays, and Addresses. By Samuel A. Barnett, Warden of Toynbee Hall, Whitechapel; Canon of Bristol Cathedral; Select Preacher before Oxford University. *Crown 8vo. 6s.*

Bathe.—Works by the Rev. Anthony Bathe, M.A.
    A LENT WITH JESUS. A Plain Guide for Churchmen. Containing Readings for Lent and Easter Week, and on the Holy Eucharist. *32mo, 1s.; or in paper cover, 6d.*
    AN ADVENT WITH JESUS. *32mo, 1s.; or in paper cover, 6d.*
    WHAT I SHOULD BELIEVE. A Simple Manual of Self-Instruction for Church People. *Small 8vo, limp, 1s. ; cloth gilt, 2s.*

Bathe and Buckham.—THE CHRISTIAN'S ROAD BOOK. 2 Parts. By the Rev. Anthony Bathe and Rev. F. H. Buckham. Part I. DEVOTIONS. *Sewed, 6d. ; limp cloth, 1s. ; cloth extra, 1s. 6d.* Part II. READINGS. *Sewed, 1s. ; limp cloth, 2s. ; cloth extra, 3s. ; or complete in one volume, sewed, 1s. 6d. ; limp cloth, 2s. 6d. ; cloth extra, 3s. 6d.*

Benson.—Works by the Rev. R. M. BENSON, M.A., Student of Christ Church, Oxford.

THE FINAL PASSOVER: A Series of Meditations upon the Passion of our Lord Jesus Christ. *Small 8vo.*

Vol. I.—THE REJECTION. 5*s*.
Vol. II.—THE UPPER CHAMBER.
Part I. 5*s*.
Part II. 5*s*.

Vol. III.—THE DIVINE EXODUS. Parts I. and II. 5*s*. each.
Vol. IV.—THE LIFE BEYOND THE GRAVE. 5*s*.

THE MAGNIFICAT; a Series of Meditations upon the Song of the Blessed Virgin Mary. *Small 8vo. 2s.*

SPIRITUAL READINGS FOR EVERY DAY. 3 *vols. Small 8vo. 3s. 6d. each.*

I. ADVENT.   II. CHRISTMAS.   III. EPIPHANY.

BENEDICTUS DOMINUS : A Course of Meditations for Every Day of the Year. Vol. I.—ADVENT TO TRINITY. Vol. II.—TRINITY, SAINTS' DAYS, etc. *Small 8vo. 3s. 6d. each ; or in One Volume, 7s.*

BIBLE TEACHINGS : The Discourse at Capernaum.—St. John vi. *Small 8vo. 3s. 6d.*

THE WISDOM OF THE SON OF DAVID : An Exposition of the First Nine Chapters of the Book of Proverbs. *Small 8vo. 3s. 6d.*

THE MANUAL OF INTERCESSORY PRAYER. *Royal 32mo.; cloth boards, 1s. 3d. ; cloth limp, 9d.*

THE EVANGELIST LIBRARY CATECHISM. Part I. *Small 8vo. 3s.*

PAROCHIAL MISSIONS. *Small 8vo. 2s. 6d.*

Bickersteth.—YESTERDAY, TO-DAY, AND FOR EVER : a Poem in Twelve Books. By EDWARD HENRY BICKERSTETH, D.D., Lord Bishop of Exeter. *One Shilling Edition, 18mo. With red borders, 16mo, 2s. 6d.*

The Crown 8vo Edition (5s.) may still be had.

Blunt.—Works by the Rev. JOHN HENRY BLUNT, D.D.

THE ANNOTATED BOOK OF COMMON PRAYER : Being an Historical, Ritual, and Theological Commentary on the Devotional System of the Church of England. *4to. 21s.*

THE COMPENDIOUS EDITION OF THE ANNOTATED BOOK OF COMMON PRAYER : Forming a concise Commentary on the Devotional System of the Church of England. *Crown 8vo. 10s. 6d.*

DICTIONARY OF DOCTRINAL AND HISTORICAL THEOLOGY. By various Writers. *Imperial 8vo. 21s.*

DICTIONARY OF SECTS, HERESIES, ECCLESIASTICAL PARTIES AND SCHOOLS OF RELIGIOUS THOUGHT. By various Writers. *Imperial 8vo. 21s.*

THE REFORMATION OF THE CHURCH OF ENGLAND: its History, Principles, and Results. 1574-1662. *Two Vols. 8vo. 34s.*

Blunt.—Works by the Rev. JOHN HENRY BLUNT, D.D.—*contd.*
THE BOOK OF CHURCH LAW. Being an Exposition of the Legal
Rights and Duties of the Parochial Clergy and the Laity of the Church
of England. Revised by the Right Hon. Sir WALTER G. F. PHILLI-
MORE, Bart., D.C.L., and G. EDWARDES JONES, Barrister-at-Law.
Crown 8vo. 9s.
A COMPANION TO THE BIBLE: Being a Plain Commentary on
Scripture History, to the end of the Apostolic Age. *Two Vols. small
8vo. Sold separately.* OLD TEST. 3s. 6d. NEW TEST. 3s. 6d.
HOUSEHOLD THEOLOGY: a Handbook of Religious Information
respecting the Holy Bible, the Prayer Book, the Church, etc., etc.
Paper cover, 16mo. 1s. *Also the Larger Edition,* 3s. 6d.

Body.—Works by the Rev. GEORGE BODY, D.D., Canon of Durham.
THE LIFE OF LOVE. A Course of Lent Lectures. 16mo. 2s. 6d.
THE SCHOOL OF CALVARY; or, Laws of Christian Life revealed
from the Cross. 16mo. 2s. 6d.
THE LIFE OF JUSTIFICATION. 16mo. 2s. 6d.
THE LIFE OF TEMPTATION. 16mo. 2s. 6d.
THE PRESENT STATE OF THE FAITHFUL DEPARTED. *Small
8vo. sewed,* 6d. 32mo. *cloth,* 1s.

Boultbee.—A COMMENTARY ON THE THIRTY-NINE
ARTICLES OF THE CHURCH OF ENGLAND. By the Rev.
T. P. BOULTBEE, formerly Principal of the London College of Divinity,
St. John's Hall, Highbury. *Crown 8vo.* 6s.

Bright.—Works by WILLIAM BRIGHT, D.D., Regius Professor
of Ecclesiastical History in the University of Oxford,
and Canon of Christ Church, Oxford.
SOME ASPECTS OF PRIMITIVE CHURCH LIFE. *Crown 8vo.* 6s.
THE ROMAN SEE IN THE EARLY CHURCH: And other Studies
in Church History. *Crown 8vo.* 7s. 6d.
WAYMARKS IN CHURCH HISTORY. *Crown 8vo.* 7s. 6d.
LESSONS FROM THE LIVES OF THREE GREAT FATHERS.
St. Athanasius, St. Chrysostom, and St. Augustine. *Crown 8vo.* 6s.
THE INCARNATION AS A MOTIVE POWER. *Crown 8vo.* 6s.

Bright and Medd.—LIBER PRECUM PUBLICARUM EC-
CLESIÆ ANGLICANÆ. A GULIELMO BRIGHT, S.T.P., et PETRO
GOLDSMITH MEDD, A.M., Latine redditus. *Small 8vo.* 7s. 6d.

Browne.—WEARIED WITH THE BURDEN: A Book of
Daily Readings for Lent. By ARTHUR HEBER BROWNE, M.A.,
LL.D., late Rector of St. John's, Newfoundland. *Crown 8vo.* 4s. 6d.

Browne.—AN EXPOSITION OF THE THIRTY-NINE
ARTICLES, Historical and Doctrinal. By E. H. BROWNE, D.D.,
sometime Bishop of Winchester. *8vo.* 16s.

Campion and Beamont.—THE PRAYER BOOK INTER-
LEAVED. With Historical Illustrations and Explanatory Notes
arranged parallel to the Text. By W. M. CAMPION, D.D., and W. J.
BEAMONT, M.A. *Small 8vo.* 7s. 6d.

Ellicott.—Works by C. J. ELLICOTT, D.D., Bishop of Gloucester.
A CRITICAL AND GRAMMATICAL COMMENTARY ON ST.
PAUL'S EPISTLES. Greek Text, with a Critical and Grammatical
Commentary, and a Revised English Translation. *8vo.*

GALATIANS. 8s. 6d.	PHILIPPIANS, COLOSSIANS, AND
EPHESIANS. 8s. 6d.	PHILEMON. 10s. 6d.
	THESSALONIANS. 7s. 6d.

PASTORAL EPISTLES. 10s. 6d.

HISTORICAL LECTURES ON THE LIFE OF OUR LORD
JESUS CHRIST. *8vo.* 12s.

ENGLISH (THE) CATHOLIC'S VADE MECUM : a Short
Manual of General Devotion. Compiled by a PRIEST. 32mo. *limp,*
1s. ; *cloth,* 2s.

     PRIEST's Edition. 32mo. 1s. 6d.

Epochs of Church History.—Edited by Right Hon. and Right
Rev. MANDELL CREIGHTON, D.D., Lord Bishop of
London. *Small 8vo.* 2s. 6d. each.

THE ENGLISH CHURCH IN OTHER LANDS. By the Rev. H. W. TUCKER, M.A.

THE HISTORY OF THE REFORMATION IN ENGLAND. By the Rev. GEO. G. PERRY, M.A.

THE CHURCH OF THE EARLY FATHERS. By the Rev. ALFRED PLUMMER, D.D.

THE EVANGELICAL REVIVAL IN THE EIGHTEENTH CENTURY. By the Rev. J. H. OVERTON, D.D.

THE UNIVERSITY OF OXFORD. By the Hon. G. C. BRODRICK, D.C.L.

THE UNIVERSITY OF CAMBRIDGE. By J. BASS MULLINGER, M.A.

THE ENGLISH CHURCH IN THE MIDDLE AGES. By the Rev. W. HUNT, M.A.

THE CHURCH AND THE EASTERN EMPIRE. By the Rev. H. F. TOZER, M.A.

THE CHURCH AND THE ROMAN EMPIRE. By the Rev. A. CARR, M.A.

THE CHURCH AND THE PURITANS, 1570-1660. By HENRY OFFLEY WAKEMAN M.A.

HILDEBRAND AND HIS TIMES. By the Rev. W. R. W. STEPHENS, M.A.

THE POPES AND THE HOHENSTAUFEN. By UGO BALZANI.

THE COUNTER REFORMATION. By ADOLPHUS WILLIAM WARD, Litt.D.

WYCLIFFE AND MOVEMENTS FOR REFORM. By REGINALD L. POOLE, M.A.

THE ARIAN CONTROVERSY. By the Rev. H. M. GWATKIN, M.A.

EUCHARISTIC MANUAL (THE). Consisting of Instructions
and Devotions for the Holy Sacrament of the Altar. From various
sources. 32mo. *cloth gilt, red edges.* 1s. *Cheap Edition, limp cloth.* 9d.

Farrar.—Works by FREDERICK W. FARRAR, D.D., Dean of
Canterbury.

THE BIBLE : Its Meaning and Supremacy. *8vo.* 15s.

TEXTS EXPLAINED ; or, Helps to Understand the New Testament.
Crown 8vo.   [*In the press.*

ALLEGORIES. With 25 Illustrations by AMELIA BAUERLE. *Crown
8vo.* 6s.

     CONTENTS.—The Life Story of Aner—The Choice—The Fortunes of a
Royal House—The Basilisk and the Leopard.

Fosbery.—Works edited by the Rev. THOMAS VINCENT FOSBERY, M.A., sometime Vicar of St. Giles's, Reading.

VOICES OF COMFORT. *Cheap Edition. Small 8vo. 3s. 6d.*
The Larger Edition (7s. 6d.) may still be had.

HYMNS AND POEMS FOR THE SICK AND SUFFERING. In connection with the Service for the Visitation of the Sick. Selected from Various Authors. *Small 8vo. 3s. 6d.*

Geikie.—Works by J. CUNNINGHAM GEIKIE, D.D., LL.D., late Vicar of St. Martin-at-Palace, Norwich.

HOURS WITH THE BIBLE : the Scriptures in the Light of Modern Discovery and Knowledge. *New Edition, largely rewritten. Complete in Twelve Volumes. Crown 8vo. 3s. 6d. each.*

OLD TESTAMENT.

In Six Volumes. Sold separately. 3s. 6d. each.

CREATION TO THE PATRIARCHS. *With a Map and Illustrations.*

MOSES TO JUDGES. *With a Map and Illustrations.*

SAMSON TO SOLOMON. *With a Map and Illustrations.*

REHOBOAM TO HEZEKIAH. *With Illustrations.*

MANASSEH TO ZEDEKIAH. With the Contemporary Prophets. *With a Map and Illustrations.*

EXILE TO MALACHI. With the Contemporary Prophets. *With Illustrations.*

NEW TESTAMENT.

In Six Volumes. Sold separately. 3s. 6d. each.

THE GOSPELS. *With a Map and Illustrations.*

LIFE AND WORDS OF CHRIST. *With Map. 2 vols.*

LIFE AND EPISTLES OF ST. PAUL. *With Maps and Illustrations. 2 vols.*

ST. PETER TO REVELATION. *With 29 Illustrations.*

LIFE AND WORDS OF CHRIST.
Cabinet Edition. With Map. 2 vols. Post 8vo. 7s.
Cheap Edition, without the Notes. 1 vol. 8vo. 5s.

A SHORT LIFE OF CHRIST. *With Illustrations. Crown 8vo. 3s. 6d. ; gilt edges, 4s. 6d.*

OLD TESTAMENT CHARACTERS. *With Illustrations. Crown 8vo. 3s. 6d.*

LANDMARKS OF OLD TESTAMENT HISTORY. *Crown 8vo. 3s. 6d.*

THE ENGLISH REFORMATION. *Crown 8vo. 3s. 6d.*

ENTERING ON LIFE. A Book for Young Men. *Crown 8vo. 2s. 6d.*

THE PRECIOUS PROMISES. *Crown 8vo. 2s.*

GOLD DUST : a Collection of Golden Counsels for the Sanctification of Daily Life.   Translated and abridged from the French by E.L.E.E.   Edited by CHARLOTTE M. YONGE.   Parts I. II. III. Small Pocket Volumes. *Cloth, gilt, each 1s.*   Parts I. and II. in One Volume. *1s. 6d.*   Parts I., II., and III. in One Volume. *2s.*

*** The two first parts in One Volume, *large type,* 18mo. *cloth, gilt.* *2s. 6d.* Parts I. II. and III. are also supplied, bound in white cloth, with red edges, in box, price *3s.*

Gore.—Works by the Rev. CHARLES GORE, M.A., D.D., Canon of Westminster.

THE MINISTRY OF THE CHRISTIAN CHURCH. *8vo.* *10s. 6d.* ROMAN CATHOLIC CLAIMS. *Crown 8vo.* *3s. 6d.*

GREAT TRUTHS OF THE CHRISTIAN RELIGION. Edited by the Rev. W. U. RICHARDS. *Small 8vo.* *2s.*

Hall.—Works by the Right Rev. A. C. A. HALL, D.D., Bishop of Vermont.

THE VIRGIN MOTHER: Retreat Addresses on the Life of the Blessed Virgin Mary as told in the Gospels.   With an appended Essay on the Virgin Birth of our Lord. *Crown 8vo.* *4s. 6d.* CHRIST'S TEMPTATION AND OURS. *Crown 8vo.* *3s. 6d.*

Hall.—THE KENOTIC THEORY. Considered with Particular Reference to its Anglican Forms and Arguments.   By the Rev. FRANCIS J. HALL, D.D., Instructor of Dogmatic Theology in the Western Theological Seminary, Chicago, Illinois. *Crown 8vo.* *5s.*

HALLOWING OF SORROW, THE. By E. R.   With a Preface by H. S. HOLLAND, M.A., Canon and Precentor of St. Paul's. *Small 8vo.* *2s.*

Harrison.—Works by the Rev. ALEXANDER J. HARRISON, B.D., Lecturer of the Christian Evidence Society.

PROBLEMS OF CHRISTIANITY AND SCEPTICISM. *Crown 8vo.* *7s. 6d.* THE CHURCH IN RELATION TO SCEPTICS : a Conversational Guide to Evidential Work. *Crown 8vo.* *3s. 6d.* THE REPOSE OF FAITH, IN VIEW OF PRESENT DAY DIFFICULTIES. *Crown 8vo.* *7s. 6d.*

Hatch.—THE ORGANIZATION OF THE EARLY CHRISTIAN CHURCHES.   Being the Bampton Lectures for 1880. By EDWIN HATCH, M.A., D.D., late Reader in Ecclesiastical History in the University of Oxford. *8vo.* *5s.*

Heygate.—THE MANUAL : a Book of Devotion.   Adapted for General Use.   By the Rev. W. E. HEYGATE, M.A., Rector of Brighstone.   18mo. *cloth limp, 1s.* ; *boards, 1s. 3d.*   *Cheap Edition, 6d.* *Small 8vo.* *Large Type, 1s. 6d.*

Holland.—Works by the Rev. HENRY SCOTT HOLLAND, M.A., Canon and Precentor of St. Paul's.

GOD'S CITY AND THE COMING OF THE KINGDOM. *Cr. 8vo.* 3s. 6d.

PLEAS AND CLAIMS FOR CHRIST. *Crown 8vo.* 3s. 6d.

CREED AND CHARACTER : Sermons. *Crown 8vo.* 3s. 6d.

ON BEHALF OF BELIEF. Sermons. *Crown 8vo.* 3s. 6d.

CHRIST OR ECCLESIASTES. Sermons. *Crown 8vo.* 2s. 6d.

LOGIC AND LIFE, with other Sermons. *Crown 8vo.* 3s. 6d.

Hollings.—Works by the Rev. G. S. HOLLINGS, Mission Priest of the Society of St. John the Evangelist, Cowley, Oxford.

THE HEAVENLY STAIR ; or, A Ladder of the Love of God for Sinners. *Crown 8vo.* 3s. 6d.

PORTA REGALIS ; or, Considerations on Prayer. *Crown 8vo. limp cloth,* 1s. 6d. net ; cloth boards, 2s. net.

MEDITATIONS ON THE DIVINE LIFE, THE BLESSED SACRA-MENT, AND THE TRANSFIGURATION. *Crown 8vo.* 3s. 6d.

CONSIDERATIONS ON THE SPIRITUAL LIFE. Suggested by Passages in the Collects for the Sundays in Lent. *Crown 8vo.* 2s. 6d.

CONSIDERATIONS ON THE WISDOM OF GOD. *Crown 8vo.* 4s.

PARADOXES OF THE LOVE OF GOD, especially as they are seen in the way of the Evangelical Counsels. *Crown 8vo.* 4s.

ONE BORN OF THE SPIRIT ; or, the Unification of our Life in God. *Crown 8vo.* 3s. 6d.

Hutchings.—Works by the Ven. W. H. HUTCHINGS, M.A. Arch-deacon of Cleveland, Canon of York, Rector of Kirby Misperton, and Rural Dean of Malton.

SERMON SKETCHES from some of the Sunday Lessons throughout the Church's Year. *Vols. I and II. Crown 8vo.* 5s. each.

THE LIFE OF PRAYER : a Course of Lectures delivered in All Saints Church, Margaret Street, during Lent. *Crown 8vo.* 4s. 6d.

THE PERSON AND WORK OF THE HOLY GHOST : a Doctrinal and Devotional Treatise. *Crown 8vo.* 4s. 6d.

SOME ASPECTS OF THE CROSS. *Crown 8vo.* 4s. 6d.

THE MYSTERY OF THE TEMPTATION. Lent Lectures delivered a St. Mary Magdalene, Paddington. *Crown 8vo.* 4s. 6d.

Hutton.—THE CHURCH OF THE SIXTH CENTURY. Six Chapters in Ecclesiastical History. By WILLIAM HOLDEN HUTTON, B.D., Birkbeck Lecturer in Ecclesiastical History, Trinity College, Cambridge. *With 11 Illustrations. Crown 8vo. 6s.*

Hutton.—THE SOUL HERE AND HEREAFTER. By the Rev. R. E. HUTTON, Chaplain of St. Margaret's, East Grinstead. *Crown 8vo. 6s.*

INHERITANCE OF THE SAINTS ; or, Thoughts on the Communion of Saints and the Life of the World to come. Collected chiefly from English Writers by L. P. With a Preface by the Rev. HENRY SCOTT HOLLAND, M.A. *Seventh Edition. Crown 8vo. 7s. 6d.*

Jameson.—Works by Mrs. JAMESON.

SACRED AND LEGENDARY ART, containing Legends of the Angels and Archangels, the Evangelists, the Apostles. With 19 Etchings and 187 Woodcuts. *2 vols. 8vo. 20s. net.*

LEGENDS OF THE MONASTIC ORDERS, as represented in the Fine Arts. With 11 Etchings and 88 Woodcuts. *8vo. 10s. net.*

LEGENDS OF THE MADONNA, OR BLESSED VIRGIN MARY. With 27 Etchings and 165 Woodcuts. *8vo. 10s. net.*

THE HISTORY OF OUR LORD, as exemplified in Works of Art. Commenced by the late Mrs. JAMESON ; continued and completed by LADY EASTLAKE. With 31 Etchings and 281 Woodcuts. *2 Vols. 8vo. 20s. net.*

Jennings.—ECCLESIA ANGLICANA. A History of the Church of Christ in England from the Earliest to the Present Times. By the Rev. ARTHUR CHARLES JENNINGS, M.A. *Crown 8vo. 7s. 6d.*

Jukes.—Works by ANDREW JUKES.

THE NEW MAN AND THE ETERNAL LIFE. Notes on the Reiterated Amens of the Son of God. *Crown 8vo. 6s.*

THE NAMES OF GOD IN HOLY SCRIPTURE : a Revelation of His Nature and Relationships. *Crown 8vo. 4s. 6d.*

THE TYPES OF GENESIS. *Crown 8vo. 7s. 6d.*

THE SECOND DEATH AND THE RESTITUTION OF ALL THINGS. *Crown 8vo. 3s. 6d.*

THE ORDER AND CONNEXION OF THE CHURCH'S TEACHING, as set forth in the arrangement of the Epistles and Gospels throughout the Year. *Crown 8vo. 2s. 6d.*

THE CHRISTIAN HOME. *Crown 8vo. 3s. 6d.*

Knox Little.—Works by W. J. KNOX LITTLE, M.A., Canon Residentiary of Worcester, and Vicar of Hoar Cross.

THE PERFECT LIFE : Sermons. *Crown 8vo. 7s. 6d.*

CHARACTERISTICS AND MOTIVES OF THE CHRISTIAN LIFE. Ten Sermons preached in Manchester Cathedral, in Lent and Advent. *Crown 8vo. 2s. 6d.*

SERMONS PREACHED FOR THE MOST PART IN MANCHESTER. *Crown 8vo. 3s. 6d.*

THE MYSTERY OF THE PASSION OF OUR MOST HOLY REDEEMER. *Crown 8vo. 2s. 6d.*

THE LIGHT OF LIFE. Sermons preached on Various Occasions. *Crown 8vo. 3s. 6d.*

SUNLIGHT AND SHADOW IN THE CHRISTIAN LIFE. Sermons preached for the most part in America. *Crown 8vo. 3s. 6d.*

Lear.—Works by, and Edited by, H. L. SIDNEY LEAR.

FOR DAYS AND YEARS. A book containing a Text, Short Reading, and Hymn for Every Day in the Church's Year. *16mo. 2s. 6d. Also a Cheap Edition, 32mo. 1s.; or cloth gilt, 1s. 6d.; or with red borders, 2s. 6d.*

FIVE MINUTES. Daily Readings of Poetry. *16mo. 3s. 6d. Also a Cheap Edition, 32mo. 1s.; or cloth gilt, 1s. 6d.*

WEARINESS. A Book for the Languid and Lonely. *Large Type. Small 8vo. 5s.*

JOY: A FRAGMENT. With a slight sketch of the Author's life. *Small 8vo. 2s. 6d.*

CHRISTIAN BIOGRAPHIES. *Nine Vols. Crown 8vo. 3s. 6d. each.*

MADAME LOUISE DE FRANCE, Daughter of Louis XV., known also as the Mother Térèse de St. Augustin.

A DOMINICAN ARTIST : a Sketch of the Life of the Rev. Père Besson, of the Order of St. Dominic.

HENRI PERREYVE. By PÈRE GRATRY.

ST. FRANCIS DE SALES, Bishop and Prince of Geneva.

THE REVIVAL OF PRIESTLY LIFE IN THE SEVENTEENTH CENTURY IN FRANCE.

A CHRISTIAN PAINTER OF THE NINETEENTH CENTURY.

BOSSUET AND HIS CONTEMPORARIES.

FÉNELON, ARCHBISHOP OF CAMBRAI.

HENRI DOMINIQUE LACORDAIRE.

[continued.

Lear. — Works by, and Edited by, H. L. SIDNEY LEAR — *continued.*

DEVOTIONAL WORKS. Edited by H. L. SIDNEY LEAR. *New and Uniform Editions. Nine Vols.* 16mo. 2s. 6d. each.

FÉNELON'S SPIRITUAL LETTERS TO MEN.

FÉNELON'S SPIRITUAL LETTERS TO WOMEN.

A SELECTION FROM THE SPIRITUAL LETTERS OF ST. FRANCIS DE SALES. Also *Cheap Edition,* 32mo, 6d. *cloth limp;* 1s. *cloth boards.*

THE SPIRIT OF ST. FRANCIS DE SALES.

THE HIDDEN LIFE OF THE SOUL.

THE LIGHT OF THE CONSCIENCE. Also *Cheap Edition,* 32mo, 6d. *cloth limp;* and 1s. *cloth boards.*

SELF-RENUNCIATION. From the French.

ST. FRANCIS DE SALES' OF THE LOVE OF GOD.

SELECTIONS FROM PASCAL'S 'THOUGHTS.'

Lepine. — THE MINISTERS OF JESUS CHRIST : a Biblical Study. By J. FOSTER LEPINE, Curate of St. Paul's, Maidstone. *Crown 8vo.* 5s.

Liddon. — Works by HENRY PARRY LIDDON, D.D., D.C.L., LL.D.

SERMONS ON SOME WORDS OF ST. PAUL. *Crown 8vo.* 5s.

SERMONS PREACHED ON SPECIAL OCCASIONS, 1860-1889. *Crown 8vo.* 5s.

EXPLANATORY ANALYSIS OF ST. PAUL'S FIRST EPISTLE TO TIMOTHY. *8vo.* 7s. 6d.

CLERICAL LIFE AND WORK : Sermons. *Crown 8vo.* 5s.

ESSAYS AND ADDRESSES : Lectures on Buddhism—Lectures on the Life of St. Paul—Papers on Dante. *Crown 8vo.* 5s.

EXPLANATORY ANALYSIS OF ST. PAUL'S FIRST EPISTLE TO TIMOTHY. *8vo.* 7s. 6d.

EXPLANATORY ANALYSIS OF PAUL'S EPISTLE TO THE ROMANS. *8vo.* 14s.

SERMONS ON OLD TESTAMENT SUBJECTS. *Crown 8vo.* 5s.

SERMONS ON SOME WORDS OF CHRIST. *Crown 8vo.* 5s.

THE DIVINITY OF OUR LORD AND SAVIOUR JESUS CHRIST. Being the Bampton Lectures for 1866. *Crown 8vo.* 5s.

ADVENT IN ST. PAUL'S. *Two Vols. Crown 8vo.* 3s. 6d. each. *Cheap Edition in one Volume. Crown 8vo.* 5s.

CHRISTMASTIDE IN ST. PAUL'S. *Crown 8vo.* 5s.

PASSIONTIDE SERMONS. *Crown 8vo.* 5s.

EASTER IN ST. PAUL'S. Sermons bearing chiefly on the Resurrection of our Lord. *Two Vols. Crown 8vo.* 3s. 6d. each. *Cheap Edition in one Volume. Crown 8vo.* 5s.

SERMONS PREACHED BEFORE THE UNIVERSITY OF OXFORD. *Two Vols. Crown 8vo.* 3s. 6d. each. *Cheap Edition in one Volume. Crown 8vo.* 5s.

[continued.

Liddon.—Works by HENRY PARRY LIDDON, D.D., D.C.L., LL.D.—*continued.*

THE MAGNIFICAT. Sermons in St. Paul's. *Crown 8vo.* 2s. 6d.

SOME ELEMENTS OF RELIGION. Lent Lectures. *Small 8vo.* 2s. 6d. [*The Crown 8vo. Edition* (5s.) *may still be had.*]

SELECTIONS FROM THE WRITINGS OF. *Crown 8vo.* 3s. 6d.

MAXIMS AND GLEANINGS. *Crown 16mo.* 1s.

Linklater.—TRUE LIMITS OF RITUAL IN THE CHURCH. Edited by Rev. ROBERT LINKLATER, D.D., Vicar of Stroud Green. *Crown 8vo.* 5s.

CONTENTS.—Preface—Introductory Essay, by the Rev. ROBERT LINK-LATER, D.D.—The Ornaments Rubric, by J. T. MICKLETHWAITE, V.P.S.A.—The Catholic Principle of Conformity in Divine Worship, by the Rev. C. F. G. TURNER—A Plea for Reasonableness, by the Rev. JOHN WYLDE—Intelligible Ritual, by the Rev. HENRY ARNOTT—The English Liturgy, by the Rev. T. A. LACEY—Eucharistic Ritual, by the Rev. W. F. COBB, D.D.—Suggestions for a Basis of Agreement in Matters Liturgical and Ceremonial, by the Rev. H. E. HALL.

Luckock.—Works by HERBERT MORTIMER LUCKOCK, D.D., Dean of Lichfield.

THE HISTORY OF MARRIAGE, JEWISH AND CHRISTIAN, IN RELATION TO DIVORCE AND CERTAIN FORBIDDEN DEGREES. *Second Edition. Crown 8vo.* 6s.

AFTER DEATH. An Examination of the Testimony of Primitive Times respecting the State of the Faithful Dead, and their Relationship to the Living. *Crown 8vo.* 3s. 6d.

THE INTERMEDIATE STATE BETWEEN DEATH AND JUDGMENT. Being a Sequel to *After Death. Crown 8vo.* 3s. 6d.

FOOTPRINTS OF THE SON OF MAN, as traced by St. Mark. Being Eighty Portions for Private Study, Family Reading, and Instruction in Church. *Crown 8vo.* 3s. 6d.

FOOTPRINTS OF THE APOSTLES, as traced by St. Luke in the Acts. Being Sixty Portions for Private Study, and Instruction in Church. A Sequel to ' Footprints of the Son of Man, as traced by St. Mark.' *Two Vols. Crown 8vo.* 12s.

THE DIVINE LITURGY. Being the Order for Holy Communion, Historically, Doctrinally, and Devotionally set forth, in Fifty Portions. *Crown 8vo.* 3s. 6d.

STUDIES IN THE HISTORY OF THE BOOK OF COMMON PRAYER. The Anglican Reform—The Puritan Innovations—The Elizabethan Reaction—The Caroline Settlement. With Appendices. *Crown 8vo.* 3s. 6d.

THE BISHOPS IN THE TOWER. A Record of Stirring Events affecting the Church and Nonconformists from the Restoration to the Revolution. *Crown 8vo.* 3s. 6d.

MacColl.—Works by the Rev. MALCOLM MacCOLL, D.D., Canon Residentiary of Ripon.
THE REFORMATION SETTLEMENT: Examined in the Light of History and Law. With an Introductory Letter to the Right Hon. W. V. Harcourt, M.P. *Crown 8vo.*
CHRISTIANITY IN RELATION TO SCIENCE AND MORALS. *Crown 8vo. 6s.*
LIFE HERE AND HEREAFTER : Sermons. *Crown 8vo. 7s. 6d.*

Mason.—Works by A. J. MASON, D.D., Lady Margaret Professor of Divinity in the University of Cambridge and Canon of Canterbury.
THE CONDITIONS OF OUR LORD'S LIFE UPON EARTH. Being the Bishop Paddock Lectures, 1896. To which is prefixed part of a First Professorial Lecture at Cambridge. *Crown 8vo. 5s.*
THE PRINCIPLES OF ECCLESIASTICAL UNITY. Four Lectures delivered in St. Asaph Cathedral. *Crown 8vo. 3s. 6d.*
THE FAITH OF THE GOSPEL. A Manual of Christian Doctrine. *Crown 8vo. 7s. 6d. Cheap Edition. Crown 8vo. 3s. 6d.*
THE RELATION OF CONFIRMATION TO BAPTISM. As taught in Holy Scripture and the Fathers. *Crown 8vo. 7s. 6d.*

Maturin.—Works by the Rev. B. W. MATURIN.
SOME PRINCIPLES AND PRACTICES OF THE SPIRITUAL LIFE. *Crown 8vo. 4s. 6d.*
PRACTICAL STUDIES ON THE PARABLES OF OUR LORD. *Crown 8vo. 5s.*

Medd.—THE PRIEST TO THE ALTAR ; or, Aids to the Devout Celebration of Holy Communion, chiefly after the Ancient English Use of Sarum. By PETER GOLDSMITH MEDD, M.A., Canon of St. Alban's. Fourth Edition, revised and enlarged. *Royal 8vo. 15s.*

Meyrick.—THE DOCTRINE OF THE CHURCH OF ENGLAND ON THE HOLY COMMUNION RESTATED AS A GUIDE AT THE PRESENT TIME. By the Rev. F. MEYRICK, M.A. *Crown 8vo. 4s. 6d.*

Mortimer.—Works by the Rev. A. G. MORTIMER, D.D., Rector of St. Mark's, Philadelphia.

JESUS AND THE RESURRECTION: Thirty Addresses for Good Friday and Easter. *Crown 8vo. 5s.*

CATHOLIC FAITH AND PRACTICE: A Manual of Theology. Two Parts. *Crown 8vo.* Sold separately. Part I. *7s. 6d.* Part II. *9s.*

HELPS TO MEDITATION: Sketches for Every Day in the Year.
Vol. I. ADVENT to TRINITY. *8vo. 7s. 6d.*
Vol. II. TRINITY to ADVENT. *8vo. 7s. 6d.*

STORIES FROM GENESIS: Sermons for Children. *Crown 8vo. 4s.*

THE LAWS OF HAPPINESS ; or, The Beatitudes as teaching our Duty to God, Self, and our Neighbour. *18mo. 2s.*

THE LAWS OF PENITENCE: Addresses on the Words of our Lord from the Cross. *16mo. 1s. 6d.*

SERMONS IN MINIATURE FOR EXTEMPORE PREACHERS: Sketches for Every Sunday and Holy Day of the Christian Year. *Cr. 8vo. 6s.*

NOTES ON THE SEVEN PENITENTIAL PSALMS, chiefly from Patristic Sources. *Fcp. 8vo. 3s. 6d.*

THE SEVEN LAST WORDS OF OUR MOST HOLY REDEEMER: with Meditations on some Scenes in His Passion. *Crown 8vo. 5s.*

LEARN OF JESUS CHRIST TO DIE : Addresses on the Words of our Lord from the Cross, taken as Teaching the way of Preparation for Death. *16mo. 2s.*

Mozley.—Works by J. B. MOZLEY, D.D., late Canon of Christ Church, and Regius Professor of Divinity at Oxford.

ESSAYS, HISTORICAL AND THEO-LOGICAL. *Two Vols. 8vo.* 24s.
EIGHT LECTURES ON MIRACLES. Being the Bampton Lectures for 1865. *Crown 8vo.* 3s. 6d.
RULING IDEAS IN EARLY AGES AND THEIR RELATION TO OLD TESTAMENT FAITH. *8vo.* 6s.

SERMONS PREACHED BEFORE THE UNIVERSITY OF OX-FORD, and on Various Occasions. *Crown 8vo.* 3s. 6d.
SERMONS, PAROCHIAL AND OCCASIONAL. *Crown 8vo.* 3s. 6d.
A REVIEW OF THE BAPTISMAL CONTROVERSY. *Crown 8vo.* 3s. 6d.

Newbolt.—Works by the Rev. W. C. E. NEWBOLT, M.A., Canon and Chancellor of St. Paul's Cathedral.

RELIGION. *Crown 8vo.* 5s. (*The Oxford Library of Practical Theology.*)

PRIESTLY IDEALS; being a Course of Practical Lectures delivered in St. Paul's Cathedral to 'Our Society' and other Clergy, in Lent, 1898. *Crown 8vo.* 3s. 6d.

THE GOSPEL OF EXPERIENCE ; or, the Witness of Human Life to the truth of Revelation. Being the Boyle Lectures for 1895. *Crown 8vo.* 5s.

COUNSELS OF FAITH AND PRACTICE : being Sermons preached on various occasions. *New and Enlarged Edition. Crown 8vo.* 5s.

SPECULUM SACERDOTUM ; or, the Divine Model of the Priestly Life. *Crown 8vo.* 7s. 6d.

THE FRUIT OF THE SPIRIT. Being Ten Addresses bearing on the Spiritual Life. *Crown 8vo.* 2s. 6d.

THE MAN OF GOD. *Small 8vo.* 1s. 6d.

THE PRAYER BOOK : Its Voice and Teaching. *Crown 8vo.* 2s. 6d.

Newman.—Works by JOHN HENRY NEWMAN, B.D., sometime Vicar of St. Mary's, Oxford.

LETTERS AND CORRESPONDENCE OF JOHN HENRY NEW-MAN DURING HIS LIFE IN THE ENGLISH CHURCH. With a brief Autobiography. Edited, at Cardinal Newman's request, by ANNE MOZLEY. *2 vols. Crown 8vo.* 7s.

PAROCHIAL AND PLAIN SERMONS. *Eight Vols. Cabinet Edition. Crown 8vo.* 5s. *each. Cheaper Edition.* 3s. 6d. *each.*

SELECTION, ADAPTED TO THE SEASONS OF THE ECCLE-SIASTICAL YEAR, from the 'Parochial and Plain Sermons,' *Cabinet Edition. Crown 8vo.* 5s. *Cheaper Edition.* 3s. 6d.

FIFTEEN SERMONS PREACHED BEFORE THE UNIVERSITY OF OXFORD *Cabinet Edition. Crown 8vo.* 5s. *Cheaper Edition.* 3s. 6d.

SERMONS BEARING UPON SUBJECTS OF THE DAY. *Cabinet Edition. Crown 8vo.* 5s. *Cheaper Edition. Crown 8vo.* 3s. 6d.

LECTURES ON THE DOCTRINE OF JUSTIFICATION. *Cabinet Edition. Crown 8vo.* 5s. *Cheaper Edition.* 3s. 6d.

⁎⁎ A Complete List of Cardinal Newman's Works can be had on Application.

Osborne.—Works by EDWARD OSBORNE, Mission Priest of the Society of St. John the Evangelist, Cowley, Oxford.

THE CHILDREN'S SAVIOUR. Instructions to Children on the Life of Our Lord and Saviour Jesus Christ. *Illustrated.* 16mo. 2s. 6d.

THE SAVIOUR KING. Instructions to Children on Old Testament Types and Illustrations of the Life of Christ. *Illustrated.* 16mo. 2s. 6d.

THE CHILDREN'S FAITH. Instructions to Children on the Apostles' Creed. *Illustrated.* 16mo. 2s. 6d.

Ottley.—ASPECTS OF THE OLD TESTAMENT: being the Bampton Lectures for 1897. By ROBERT LAWRENCE OTTLEY, M.A., Vicar of Winterbourne Bassett, Wilts; sometime Principal of the Pusey House. 8vo. *New and Cheaper Edition.* 7s. 6d.

The Oxford Library of Practical Theology.

PRODUCED UNDER THE EDITORSHIP OF

The Rev. W. C. E. NEWBOLT, M.A., Canon and Chancellor of St. Paul's, and the Rev. F. E. BRIGHTMAN, M.A., Librarian of the Pusey House, Oxford.

The Price of each Volume will be Five Shillings.

The following is a list of Volumes as at present arranged :—

1. RELIGION. By the Rev. W. C. E. NEWBOLT, M.A., Canon and Chancellor of St. Paul's. *Crown 8vo.* 5s.

2. BAPTISM. By the Rev. DARWELL STONE, M.A., Principal of the Missionary College, Dorchester. *Crown 8vo.* 5s. [*In the press.*

3. CONFIRMATION. By the Right Rev. A. C. A. HALL, D.D., Bishop of Vermont.

4. HOLY MATRIMONY. By the Rev. W. J. KNOX LITTLE, M.A., Canon of Worcester.

5. THE HOLY COMMUNION. By the Rev. F. W. PULLER, M.A., Mission Priest of St. John Evangelist, Cowley.

6. THE PRAYER BOOK. By the Rev. LEIGHTON PULLAN, M.A., Fellow of St. John's College, Oxford.

7. RELIGIOUS CEREMONIAL. By the Rev. F. E. BRIGHTMAN, M.A., Librarian of the Pusey House, Oxford.

8. PRAYER. By the Rev. A. J. WORLLEDGE, M.A., Canon of Truro.

9. VISITATION OF THE SICK. By the Rev. E. F. RUSSELL, M.A., St. Alban's, Holborn.

CONFESSION and ABSOLUTION. FASTING and ALMSGIVING. RETREATS, MISSIONS, ETC. CHURCH WORK. DEVOTIONAL BOOKS and READING. ORDINATION. FOREIGN MISSIONS. THE BIBLE.

OUTLINES OF CHURCH TEACHING : a Series of Instructions for the Sundays and chief Holy Days of the Christian Year. For the Use of Teachers. By C. C. G. With Preface by the Very Rev. FRANCIS PAGET, D.D., Dean of Christ Church, Oxford. *Crown 8vo.* 3s. 6d.

Oxenham.—THE VALIDITY OF PAPAL CLAIMS : Lectures delivered in Rome. By F. NUTCOMBE OXENHAM, D.D., English Chaplain at Rome. With a Letter by His Grace the ARCHBISHOP OF YORK. *Crown 8vo.* 2s. 6d.

Paget.—Works by FRANCIS PAGET, D.D., Dean of Christ Church.

STUDIES IN THE CHRISTIAN CHARACTER: Sermons. With an Introductory Essay. *Crown 8vo.* 6s. 6d.

THE SPIRIT OF DISCIPLINE : Sermons. *Crown 8vo.* 6s. 6d.

FACULTIES AND DIFFICULTIES FOR BELIEF AND DISBELIEF. *Crown 8vo.* 6s. 6d.

THE HALLOWING OF WORK. Addresses given at Eton, January 16-18, 1888. *Small 8vo.* 2s.

Percival.—SOME HELPS FOR SCHOOL LIFE. Sermons preached at Clifton College, 1862-1879. By J. PERCIVAL, D.D., LL.D., Lord Bishop of Hereford. New Edition, with New Preface. *Crown 8vo.* 3s. 6d.

Percival.—THE INVOCATION OF SAINTS. Treated Theologically and Historically. By HENRY R. PERCIVAL, M.A., D.D., Author of 'A Digest of Theology,' 'The Doctrine of the Episcopal Church,' etc. *Crown 8vo.* 5s.

POCKET MANUAL OF PRAYERS FOR THE HOURS, ETC. With the Collects from the Prayer Book. *Royal 32mo.* 1s.

Powell.—THE PRINCIPLE OF THE INCARNATION. With especial Reference to the Relation between our Lord's Divine Omniscience and His Human Consciousness. By the Rev. H. C. POWELL, M.A. of Oriel College, Oxford ; Rector of Wylye and Prebendary of Salisbury Cathedral. *8vo.* 16s.

PRACTICAL REFLECTIONS. By a CLERGYMAN. With Prefaces by H. P. LIDDON, D.D., D.C.L., and the LORD BISHOP OF LINCOLN. *Crown 8vo.*

THE BOOK OF GENESIS. 4s. 6d.
THE PSALMS. 5s.
ISAIAH. 4s. 6d.
THE MINOR PROPHETS. 4s. 6d.
THE HOLY GOSPELS. 4s. 6d.
ACTS TO REVELATION. 6s.

PRIEST'S PRAYER BOOK (THE). Containing Private Prayers and Intercessions ; Occasional, School, and Parochial Offices ; Offices for the Visitation of the Sick, with Notes, Readings, Collects, Hymns, Litanies, etc. With a brief Pontifical. By the late Rev. R. F. LITTLEDALE, LL.D., D.C.L., and Rev. J. EDWARD VAUX, M.A., F.S.A. *New Edition, Revised. 20th Thousand. Post 8vo.* 6s. 6d.

Pullan.—LECTURES ON RELIGION. By the Rev. LEIGHTON PULLAN, M.A., Fellow of St. John's College, Lecturer in Theology at Oriel and Queen's Colleges, Oxford. *Crown 8vo.* 6*s.*

Pusey.—SPIRITUAL LETTERS OF EDWARD BOUVERIE PUSEY, D.D. Edited and prepared for publication by the Rev. J. O. JOHNSTON, M.A., Principal of the Theological College, Cuddesdon ; and the Rev. W. C. E. NEWBOLT, M.A., Canon and Chancellor of St. Paul's. *8vo.* 12*s.* 6*d.*

Randolph.—Works by B. W. RANDOLPH, M.A., Principal of the Theological College and Hon. Canon of Ely.

MEDITATIONS ON THE OLD TESTAMENT for Every Day in the Year. *Crown 8vo.* 6*s.*

THE THRESHOLD OF THE SANCTUARY : being Short Chapters on the Inner Preparation for the Priesthood. *Crown 8vo.* 3*s.* 6*d.*

THE LAW OF SINAI : being Devotional Addresses on the Ten Commandments delivered to Ordinands. *Crown 8vo.* 3*s.* 6*d.*

Rede.—Works by WYLLYS REDE, D.D., Rector of the Church of the Incarnation, and Canon of the Cathedral, Atalanta, Georgia.

STRIVING FOR THE MASTERY : Daily Lessons for Lent. *Cr. 8vo.* 5*s.*

THE COMMUNION OF SAINTS : a Lost Link in the Chain of the Church's Creed. With a Preface by LORD HALIFAX. *Crown 8vo.* 3*s.* 6*d.*

Reynolds.—THE SUPERNATURAL IN NATURE : A Verification by Free Use of Science. By JOSEPH WILLIAM REYNOLDS, M.A., Late President of Sion College, and Prebendary of St. Paul's Cathedral. *New and Cheaper Edition, Revised. Crown 8vo.* 3*s.* 6*d.*

Sanday.—Works by W. SANDAY, D.D., Margaret Professor of Divinity and Canon of Christ Church, Oxford.

THE CONCEPTION OF PRIESTHOOD IN THE EARLY CHURCH AND IN THE CHURCH OF ENGLAND : Four Sermons. *Crown 8vo.* 3*s.* 6*d.*

INSPIRATION : Eight Lectures on the Early History and Origin o the Doctrine of Biblical Inspiration. Being the Bampton Lectures for 1893. *New and Cheaper Edition, with New Preface. 8vo.* 7*s.* 6*d.*

Scudamore.—STEPS TO THE ALTAR: a Manual of Devotion for the Blessed Eucharist. By the Rev. W. E. SCUDAMORE, M.A. *Royal 32mo.* 1*s.*

On toned paper, with red rubrics, 2s : The same, with Collects, Epistles, and Gospels, 2s. 6d ; Demy 18mo. cloth, 1s ; Demy 18mo. cloth, large type, 1s. 3d ; Imperial 32mo. limp cloth, 6d.

Simpson.—THE CHURCH AND THE BIBLE. By the Rev.
W. J. SPARROW SIMPSON, M.A. Vicar of St. Mark's, Regent's Park.
Crown 8vo. 3s. 6d.
MEMOIR OF THE REV. W. SPARROW SIMPSON, D.D., Sub-
Dean of St. Paul's Cathedral. Compiled and Edited by W. J.
SPARROW SIMPSON. With Portrait and other Illustrations. *Crown
8vo. 4s. 6d.*

Strange.—INSTRUCTIONS ON THE REVELATION OF
ST. JOHN THE DIVINE: Being an attempt to make this book
more intelligible to the ordinary reader and so to encourage the study
of it. By Rev. CRESSWELL STRANGE, M.A., Vicar of Edgbaston, and
Honorary Canon of Worcester. *Crown 8vo. 6s.*

Strong.—CHRISTIAN ETHICS : being the Bampton Lectures
for 1895. By THOMAS B. STRONG, B.D., Student of Christ Church,
Oxford, and Examining Chaplain to the Lord Bishop of Durham.
New and Cheaper Edition. 8vo. 7s. 6d.

Tee.—THE SANCTUARY OF SUFFERING. By ELEANOR
TEE, Author of 'This Everyday Life,' etc. With a Preface by the
Rev. J. P. F. DAVIDSON, M.A., Vicar of St. Matthias', Earl's Court;
President of the 'Guild of All Souls.' *Crown 8vo. 7s. 6d.*

Whishaw.—THE CHILDREN'S YEAR-BOOK OF PRAYER
AND PRAISE. By C. M. WHISHAW, Compiler of 'Being and
Doing.' *Crown 8vo. 3s. 6d.*

Williams.—Works by the Rev. ISAAC WILLIAMS, B.D.
A DEVOTIONAL COMMENTARY ON THE GOSPEL NARRA-
TIVE. *Eight Vols. Crown 8vo. 5s. each.*

THOUGHTS ON THE STUDY OF THE HOLY GOSPELS.	OUR LORD'S MINISTRY (Third Year).
A HARMONY OF THE FOUR GOSPELS.	THE HOLY WEEK.
OUR LORD'S NATIVITY.	OUR LORD'S PASSION.
OUR LORD'S MINISTRY (Second Year).	OUR LORD'S RESURRECTION.

FEMALE CHARACTERS OF HOLY SCRIPTURE. A Series ot
Sermons. *Crown 8vo. 5s.*
THE CHARACTERS OF THE OLD TESTAMENT. *Crown 8vo. 5s.*
THE APOCALYPSE. With Notes and Reflections. *Crown 8vo. 5s.*
SERMONS ON THE EPISTLES AND GOSPELS FOR THE SUN-
DAYS AND HOLY DAYS. *Two Vols. Crown 8vo. 5s. each.*
PLAIN SERMONS ON CATECHISM. *Two Vols. Cr. 8vo. 5s. each.*

Wilson.—THOUGHTS ON CONFIRMATION. By Rev. R.
J. WILSON, D.D., late Warden of Keble College. *16mo. 1s. 6d.*

Wirgman.—Works by A. THEODORE WIRGMAN, B.D., D.C.L.,
Vice-Provost of St. Mary's Collegiate Church, Port Eliza-
beth, South Africa.
THE DOCTRINE OF CONFIRMATION. *Crown 8vo. 7s. 6d.*
THE CONSTITUTIONAL AUTHORITY OF BISHOPS IN THE
CATHOLIC CHURCH. Illustrated by the History and Canon Law
of the Undivided Church from the Apostolic Age to the Council of
Chalcedon, A.D. 451. *Crown 8vo. 6s.*

Wood.—THE STORY OF A SAINTLY BISHOP'S LIFE—
LANCELOT ANDREWES, Bishop of Winchester, 1555-1626. By
Lady Mary Wood. *Crown 8vo. 1s. 6d.*

Wordsworth.—Works by CHRISTOPHER WORDSWORTH, D.D.,
sometime Bishop of Lincoln.

THE HOLY BIBLE (the Old Testament). With Notes, Introductions,
and Index. *Imperial 8vo.*
Vol. I. THE PENTATEUCH. 25*s*. Vol. II. JOSHUA TO SAMUEL. 15*s*.
Vol. III. KINGS to ESTHER. 15*s*. Vol. IV. JOB TO SONG OF
SOLOMON. 25*s*. Vol. V. ISAIAH TO EZEKIEL. 25*s*. Vol. VI.
DANIEL, MINOR PROPHETS, and Index. 15*s*.
Also supplied in 12 Parts. Sold separately.

THE NEW TESTAMENT, in the Original Greek. With Notes, Intro-
ductions, and Indices. *Imperial 8vo.*
Vol. I. GOSPELS AND ACTS OF THE APOSTLES. 23*s*. Vol. II.
EPISTLES, APOCALYPSE, and Indices. 37*s*.
Also supplied in 4 Parts. Sold separately.

A CHURCH HISTORY TO A.D. 451. *Four Vols. Crown 8vo.*
Vol. I. TO THE COUNCIL OF NICÆA, A.D. 325. 8*s. 6d.* Vol. II.
FROM THE COUNCIL OF NICÆA TO THAT OF CONSTANTINOPLE
6*s*. Vol. III. CONTINUATION. 6*s*. Vol. IV. CONCLUSION, TO
THE COUNCIL OF CHALCEDON, A.D. 451. 6*s*.

THEOPHILUS ANGLICANUS: a Manual of Instruction on the
Church and the Anglican Branch of it. *12mo. 2s. 6d.*

ELEMENTS OF INSTRUCTION ON THE CHURCH. *16mo.
1s. cloth. 6d. sewed.*

THE HOLY YEAR: Original Hymns. *16mo. 2s. 6d. and 1s. Limp, 6d.*
   „   „   With Music. Edited by W. H. MONK. *Square 8vo. 4s. 6d.*

ON THE INTERMEDIATE STATE OF THE SOUL AFTER
DEATH. *32mo. 1s.*

Wordsworth.—Works by JOHN WORDSWORTH, D.D., Lord
Bishop of Salisbury.

THE EPISCOPATE OF CHARLES WORDSWORTH, D.D., D.C.L.,
Bishop of St. Andrews. With Two Portraits. *8vo. 15s.*

THE HOLY COMMUNION: Four Visitation Addresses. 1891.
Crown 8vo. 3s. 6d.

THE ONE RELIGION: Truth, Holiness, and Peace desired by the
Nations, and revealed by Jesus Christ. Eight Lectures delivered before
the University of Oxford in 1881. *Second Edition. Crown 8vo. 7s. 6d.*

UNIVERSITY SERMONS ON GOSPEL SUBJECTS. *Sm. 8vo. 2s. 6d.*

PRAYERS FOR USE IN COLLEGE. *16mo. 1s.*

5000/4/99.

Printed by T. and A. CONSTABLE, Printers to Her Majesty
at the Edinburgh University Press.

www.ingramcontent.com/pod-product-compliance
Lightning Source LLC
Chambersburg PA
CBHW020616030726
47497CB00007B/2267